D0581381

The *Oxford Progressive English Readers* series provides a wide range of reading for learners of English.

Each book in the series has been written to follow the strict guidelines of a syllabus, wordlist and structure list. The texts are graded according to these guidelines; Grade 1 at a 1,400 word level, Grade 2 at a 2,100 word level, Grade 3 at a 3,100 word level, Grade 4 at a 3,700 word level and Grade 5 at a 5,000 word level.

The latest methods of text analysis, using specially designed software, ensure that readability is carefully controlled at every level. Any new words which are vital to the mood and style of the story are explained within the text, and reoccur throughout for maximum reinforcement. New language items are also clarified by attractive illustrations.

Each book has a short section containing carefully graded exercises and controlled activities, which test both global and specific understa

Tales of Crime and Detection

Edited by David Foulds

Hong Kong
Oxford University Press
Oxford Singapore Tokyo

Oxford University Press

Oxford   New York
Athens   Auckland   Bangkok   Bombay
Calcutta   Cape Town   Dar es Salaam   Delhi
Florence   Hong Kong   Istanbul   Karachi
Kuala Lumpur   Madras   Madrid   Melbourne
Mexico City   Nairobi   Paris   Singapore
Taipei   Tokyo   Toronto

and associated companies in
Berlin   Ibadan

Oxford is a trade mark of Oxford University Press

First published 1992
This impression (lowest digit)
5   7   9   10   8   6   4

© Oxford University Press 1992

Illustrated by K.Y. Chan

Syllabus designer: David Foulds

Text processing and analysis by Luxfield Consultants Ltd

ISBN 0 19 585399 7 ✓

Printed in Hong Kong
Published by Oxford University Press (China) Ltd
18/F Warwick House East, Taikoo Place, 979 King's Road,
Quarry Bay, Hong Kong

CONTENTS

A TERRIBLY STRANGE BED

The gambling house

Not long after I left college, I was living in Paris with an English friend. We were both young men and Paris was an exciting city, so we led a rather wild life.

One evening, we were walking along wondering how to amuse ourselves. My friend suggested going to Frascati's, a gambling house. I had been there many times before and had won and lost small amounts of money. I only played cards there because it amused me. But now I was tired of Frascati's. It was too respectable for me.

'Why don't we go to a different sort of place,' I asked my friend, 'a place where you don't have to be well-dressed?'

My friend replied that he knew such a place not too far away. 'It is just the sort of place you will like. It is not respectable at all, from what I have heard.'

We started out for the place, and arrived there very soon afterwards. Quickly entering the house, we went upstairs and left our hats and walking sticks with a doorman. Then we went into the gambling room. There were very few people there, but they were the kind of people I had foolishly wanted to see. I had thought it would be amusing, but I knew then, immediately, that what we had come to see was not at all funny.

The room was very quiet. At the gambling table there was a pale, thin, young man with long hair, who never said a word. He only stared fiercely at the cards in front of him. A fat player with an ugly face marked on a

piece of
paper how
many times red
or black came up. He
5 also did not say a word. Then
there was an old man, dressed in rather dirty clothes,
who had lost all his money and could no longer play.
He merely stared silently at the cards of the other
players. Even the croupier's voice sounded as if he had
10 no interest in what he was doing, as he collected or
paid out money. I had come to this place to laugh, but
it made me feel like crying instead.

I was feeling quite unhappy and so, in order to forget
how I felt, I looked for something exciting to do.
15 Unfortunately, the nearest excitement was the gambling
table, and so I began to play. Even more unfortunately,
as you will soon see, I also began to win. I won so
much and so quickly that I could hardly believe it. All
the other players in the room crowded around me, and
20 whispered that the stranger was going to win more than

the house could pay. They also looked very greedily at the large amount of money in front of me.

We were playing Red and Black, a game I had played in many European cities. But I had never become a real gambler, and I only played for amusement. I always had a lot of money and never won or lost very much. I could always just laugh and go away. I had never before wanted to win so much that I would be very unhappy if I lost.

This time it was different. For the first time in my life I had gambling fever. The more I won, the more excited I became. My head felt as if I were ill with too much drink. I left everything to chance, following no plan, and I was lucky.

Soon the other players stopped playing, as the amounts I was betting were too high for them. But they all stayed to watch, breathlessly, as I played alone against the bank. I threw more and more money onto the table, and the excitement grew greater every time I won. The more I won, the more I played. With every win, fresh heaps of gold were pushed over to me. I could hear cries of surprise from the crowd. The only one who was calm all this time was my friend. After a while he came to my side and whispered to me that we should leave this place. He told me to be satisfied with what I had already won. He begged me several times to leave with him but I paid no attention. When I spoke rudely to him, he left.

The old soldier

A little later, a man dressed as a soldier was encouraging me to go on betting. He handed me two coins that had fallen to the floor, and urged me to try to break the bank. He assured me that he had never seen such luck in his whole life.

I could only think about winning, and therefore did
not notice how suspicious he looked. He called himself
an old soldier, but he did not look much like one. His
eyes were very red, and his nose was broken. His hands
5   were the dirtiest I had ever seen.

But, at the time, I did not notice all these things, and
only listened to those who told me to go on playing.
However, a quarter of an hour later the
croupier called out, 'Gentlemen, the
10 bank will close for tonight.'
All the bank's money lay
in front of me in great
heaps. It all belonged to
me now.

15 I was pushing my
hands into all this
wealth when the
old soldier gave me
some advice. 'Tie
20 it all up in your
handkerchief just
like we used to do
with bits of food in the
army. You have won
25 more than could fill any
pocket I have ever seen.
Tie up all the money and
gold, and make sure you leave nothing behind.' He
picked up another coin from the floor. 'Tie it up with
30 a strong double knot, then it will all be safe. You are
indeed a lucky man. I only wish we had been so lucky
in the war. If the enemy had shot bundles of money
like that at us … Well, there is just one thing I ask you
to do. Drink a bottle of champagne with an old soldier
35 before we say goodbye.'

'An excellent idea, my good friend,' I cried. 'A bottle of champagne! Let us drink to good luck.' We soon began to act like very old friends, shouting, 'Long live England! Long live France!' and other friendly words. We finished one bottle and I immediately called for another. That one was finished just as quickly, but now I began to feel very hot. 'My good soldier,' I cried like a madman, 'I feel quite strange. The wine you asked me to drink has set me on fire. Let us drink a third bottle to put the fire out!'

When the soldier heard me shouting like that, he shook his head. He then called out, 'Coffee!' He quickly got up and went to another room. To my surprise, everyone else who had been sitting about also got up and left. Perhaps they had all hoped to take advantage of me while I was drunk. Now they realized that some coffee would bring me back to normal again, so they did not want to wait any longer. Anyway, they all left.

A strange cup of coffee

The croupier had gone to eat his dinner in another room, and so, when the soldier returned, we were all alone in the room. He was very serious now, and explained that he had asked the lady of the house to make me some strong coffee. 'You must drink it, and then you will be well again. You must be careful. Some of the people who were gambling here tonight know that you have won a lot of money. They are all good people, of course, but sometimes they cannot stop themselves doing something bad. When you feel well again, you must get a carriage and ask the driver to take you straight home through the large, well-lit streets. That way you will arrive home safely, thanks to the advice of an honest old soldier.'

Just then the coffee arrived. My throat felt dry because I had drunk so much wine, and so I drank a whole cup at once. But immediately I felt worse than before. The whole room began to turn round and
5   round, and the soldier seemed to be jumping up and down in front of me. I could hear a terrible ringing sound in my ears, and I felt quite helpless. I stood up and had to hold on to the table for balance. I could just manage to say that I felt too ill to return home.

10   The soldier said, 'My friend, it would be better if you were to stay here for the night. You cannot walk properly. It would be mad for you to try to return home like that. The beds here are quite good. I am staying here tonight, and I think you should do the same.
15   Tomorrow you can go home in daylight and you will be completely safe.'

I felt so ill that I could only think of guarding my handkerchief full of money. I wanted to lie down somewhere and go to sleep. I accepted the soldier's
20   suggestion and, with his help, I went upstairs to the room they gave me. We then shook hands and we agreed to have breakfast together in the morning.

As soon as I was alone, I ran to the wash-bowl, drank some water from the jug, and put my head in the cold
25   water. After sitting down to calm myself, I slowly began to feel better. The bedroom was a pleasant change from the gambling room below. The lights were not so bright, and the air was cool. Already I felt much better.

But now I was thinking of all the dangers of sleeping
30   in a gambling house. However, the greater dangers of wandering about in the streets of Paris with all that money made me decide to stay there.

I made sure that the door was locked properly. I also pushed a heavy wooden box that had been under the
35   bed against it. I looked under the bed and into the

cupboard, and then examined the locks on the windows. After I had made sure of my safety, I undressed and lay down on the bed.

But, strangely, I could not sleep. I could not even close my eyes because I was still so excited. The events of the day had been so unusual. I rolled this way and that, but I could not find a comfortable position. I was wide awake. I tried to roll myself up in a little ball, like a kitten. I turned to the left and I turned to the right. It was no good; I knew I would have a sleepless night.

There were no books to read, but I knew I must find something to keep my mind busy, otherwise I would imagine all sorts of awful things. Then I would be very ill indeed in the morning.

I sat up and looked around the room. The moonlight coming through the window lit the room very brightly. I could see everything quite clearly. To pass the time, I made up a little game. I would look carefully at each object in the room and see what thoughts came into my mind. Very often, looking at something can bring back memories, but no matter how hard I looked, no thoughts came into my head. All I could do was to count the objects in the room.

The first thing was the bed I was lying on. It was very old with four big wooden posts, one at each corner. This was very unusual in Paris. The posts held up a cover which was like a roof made of some kind of cloth. All around the top there was a strip of cloth about six inches wide. There were curtains hanging from the top of the bed on all sides. They were tied open to the four posts. It was the kind of bed that our grandfathers and grandmothers used to sleep in.

Next I looked at the wash-stand. The water I had spilled before was still falling to the floor, drop by drop. The floor was made of bricks. My clothes were spread out over two small chairs. There was another old chair in one corner of the room with torn white covers. The dressing-table was broken and the mirror on it was old and dirty. On the wall hung a picture of a man wearing

5 a Spanish hat with five large feathers in it. He was looking up and so I decided that I would also look up.

Was the bed moving?

All I could see was the top of the bed, so I looked at the picture again. The feathers in the hat were long.

10 There were three white ones and two green ones. The moonlight coming through the window was quite bright.

For a while I sat on the bed quietly, not thinking about anything at all. I nearly fell asleep. Then I looked

15 back at the picture once again. There was something wrong with it. I looked harder. Something was missing.

The feathers were gone. In fact, the whole hat was gone. Had the man taken off his hat? That was impossible. Something dark was covering the man's face.

Was the bed moving?

I rolled onto my back and stared up. Was I dreaming? Had I gone mad? Was the top of the bed really coming down towards me?

I could not believe my eyes. Slowly, silently, the cover was coming down towards me. I felt ice-cold and my blood seemed to stand still. I turned my head again to look at the picture. This way I could check if the bed really was moving.

One quick look and I knew the terrible truth. Now the man's face was completely hidden. Then the whole picture was gone. I was so frightened that I could not move a muscle, and I lay on the bed waiting for the top of the bed to come all the way down. When it covered me, I knew that I would not be able to breathe. It would suffocate me.

There was now only a little light coming from the moon, but I could still see the cover moving down, closer and closer. At the last moment, like an animal trying to save its life, I rolled off. My shoulder touched the edge of the cover, but there was just enough room for me to escape.

Now I could see the top of the bed. The cover, which I had thought was just a large cloth, was really a very thick mattress. It was being pressed down hard onto the lower mattress that I had been lying on. There was not enough room for my hand to go between the two. I could see that the top mattress was moved up and down the four posts by a big wooden screw. This screw went through a hole in the ceiling to the room above. Someone must be up there, turning the screw and making the cover come down. The whole thing was a machine for murdering people. I did not think that such awful things still existed in a modern city like Paris.

5   After I had watched all this, I began to think much more clearly, and I understood what had happened to me. Something had been put into my coffee to make me fall asleep, but they had put in too much and it had had the opposite effect. I had been very foolish to trust
10   those people in the gambling house. They were criminals who wanted to kill me for my money. Then I thought of all the men who had come here just like me, and who had died in this bed. The thought made me feel very cold again.

15   After about ten minutes, the top of the bed moved up again, just as slowly and silently as it had come down. At the top neither the screw nor the hole in the ceiling could be seen. It was just an ordinary old four-poster bed again.

20   ## A lucky escape

I was able to move now, and I began to think of my escape. Quickly I put my clothes on, but I had to be absolutely quiet. If I made even the smallest noise, the murderers would hear it and try to kill me. I would not
25   be so lucky the second time. I listened but there was no sound anywhere. The box I had pushed in front of the door was still there, but I did not dare to think of what might be inside it. It could not be moved quietly, and I thought it would be too dangerous to escape
30   through the house anyway. There was only one way out — through the window.

The room was on the second floor and looked down into a small street. Slowly I crept to the window and

opened it very carefully. It took about five minutes but
it seemed like five hours. It was too high to jump to
the ground, but luckily there was a pipe beside the
window which went all the way down. I did everything
as quietly as a thief.   5

Just as I started to climb out of the window, I
remembered the money under the pillow. I did not
want those people in the house to have it even though
I did not need it. Just then I thought I heard the sound
of someone breathing outside my room. My heart   10
almost stopped but it was only the wind blowing under
the door. No one was there.

As soon as I was on the street, I ran to a police station
that I knew was not too far away. I told an officer the
story, but I was so out of breath that he thought I had   15
drunk too much wine. However, when I finished the
whole story, he believed me. Six men got ready and
we all went to the house through the quiet streets.

Two policemen stood guard at the back of the house
and the rest of us went to the front door. The officer   20
told me to hide behind another policeman, and then
knocked on the door. A light appeared at an upstairs
window and the officer shouted, 'Open up, in the name
of the law!'

A man who was only half-dressed opened the door.   25
'What do you want?'

'We want to see the Englishman who is sleeping in
this house.'

'He went away hours ago.'

'He did not go away. His friend went away but he   30
stayed. Take us to his room!'

'Honestly he —'

'He slept here,' interrupted the officer, 'but he found
the bed uncomfortable and complained to us. We want
to see it!'   35

The officers tied up the man who had opened the door, and everybody went upstairs. Everyone in the house was caught, even the 'old soldier'.

After looking at my room we went upstairs to the room above it. Everything looked very ordinary, but one of the officers knocked on the floor in a few places. One place sounded strange, and the men opened the floor there. In the floor we could see the handle which was used to turn the big screw. Some of us then went back to my room while the others lowered the bed again. I told the officer that this time it made a lot more noise. 'This is the first time my men have done it. The criminals have had a lot of practice,' explained the officer.

The rest of the story is quite simple. The 'old soldier' was the master of the gambling house. Many years before, he had been dismissed from the army for stealing. The croupier and the woman also knew about the bed. Who knows how many men had been murdered there? The three of them went to prison and the house was closed, and I became the most famous person in Paris for a whole week.

There was one very good result. I never played Red and Black again. When I see the green top of a gambling table, I always think of the top of that bed coming down to suffocate me.

THE CAVE OF ALI BABA

The newspaper article

A man was sitting in the front room of a tall, narrow house in Lambeth. He was having breakfast, and reading a newspaper which was on the table beside him. He was rather small and thin, and had brown hair. His beard was pointed. His suit, socks, tie, and handkerchief were all of the same blue colour. 5

He did not look quite like a gentleman, but he behaved like someone who has lived with a good family. He had set the breakfast table himself, and it was done just as a good servant would do it. Every detail was correct. Still, he was not old enough to be a retired servant. Perhaps he was a servant who had been left some money.

He drank his coffee while he read an article in the newspaper very carefully. The article said:

Death of Lord Peter Wimsey
Lord Peter Wimsey was killed last December while hunting wild animals in East Africa. He has left a sum of £500,000 of which £10,000 has been given to

*hospitals and societies helping the poor. Bunter, his
private servant, received £500 per year and his house
in London. All the rest of his money and everything
else that he owned went to his mother, the Duchess of
Denver.*

*Lord Peter Wimsey was thirty-seven at the time of his
death. He was a well-known private detective and
helped to solve several famous mysteries.*

'There is no doubt about it,' the man said to himself,
aloud. 'People don't give away their money if they are
going to come back again. He must be dead and buried.
And I am free!'

The first meeting

He put on his hat and went out. A bus took him to
Bermondsey. He walked for a while, and finally arrived
at a bar in a poor area of town. He went in and ordered
a whisky.

There were a number of men in the bar. When the
man reached for his glass, he knocked over another
man's drink. This man was wearing a black and white
suit. 'Here!' this man said angrily, 'What are you doing?
We don't want you in here. Get out!' He gave the man
from Lambeth a push.

The man from Lambeth replied, 'The bar is open.
Anyone can come in for a drink, can't they?' and he
pushed the man with the black and white suit in return.

The owner of the bar tried to make peace again.
'Now, stop that. The gentleman did not spill your drink
on purpose, Mr Jukes.'

'It was an accident,' added the man from Lambeth, 'I
did not plan to come in here and make trouble. But,
of course, if anybody does want to make trouble …'

'All right, all right,' said Mr Jukes more peacefully, 'We won't quarrel. Will you have a drink with me?'

'No, no, please have one with me,' answered the other man, and he ordered two whiskies.

They got their drinks. 'Let's go over there, it's not so noisy,' suggested Jukes. They went into a corner of the room.

'That was nicely done,' Mr Jukes went on, when they had sat down. 'I think there is no danger here, but one cannot be too careful. What about it, Rogers? Will you join us?' Rogers was the name of the man from Lambeth.

'Yes,' Rogers answered. He looked over his shoulder to make sure that no one was listening. 'Yes, I have decided. If it's all right. But I don't want any trouble. I don't want to do anything dangerous. I will give you some information but that is all. I don't want to take an active part in what happens. Is that clear?'

'We would not allow you to take an active part, even if you wanted to,' said Mr Jukes. 'Number One only lets the best people do jobs like this. You only have to let us know where everything is, and how to get it. The society does the rest. It is a wonderful organization, I can tell you. You won't even know who is doing it, or how it is done. You won't know anybody, and nobody will know you, except Number One. He knows everybody.'

'And you will know,' said Rogers.

'Yes of course. But I will be sent to another district. We will only meet at the general meetings. Then we all wear masks over our faces.'

'What? Are you serious?' Rogers asked unbelievingly.

'Yes. The kind of masks you might wear at a dance party. First you will be taken to Number One. You won't see his face, of course, because he will have a mask on. If he thinks that you are all right, you can join. You will be told where to send your reports. Every three months there is a general meeting. At that time you get your share of the money.'

'What happens if two people work on the same job together? Don't they see each other's faces then?'

'If it is in the daytime they will be wearing false beards or dark glasses. Even their mothers would not know them. But most of the jobs are done at night.'

'I see. But what if somebody followed me home, and then told the police about me?'

'I don't think that anyone would do that. The last man who thought of doing that was found at the bottom of the river. He did not have time to say anything to anyone. Number One knows everything that is happening.'

'Who is Number One?'

'A lot of people would like to know that, but nobody does. He has eyes all round his head. His arms reach all the way to Australia. Only Number Two knows anything about him, but I am not sure about her.'

'Are you saying there are women in the organization?'

'There certainly are. You cannot do a job without women these days. But don't worry about that. They don't want to die either, or go to prison. They think just the same as you and me.'

'But what about the money, Jukes? This work is very dangerous. Is it worth it?'

'Worth it? There are fifty members and we all get an equal share. Did you hear about the Carruthers diamonds, and the Gorleston bank robbery? Or did you hear about Lord Frensham's valuable pictures? All those jobs were done by our Society. There has never been anything like it. Number One is a great man.'

Rogers licked his lips and asked, 'What if I told the police what you have just told me?'

'You are being watched, even now. You would not get home alive.'

Rogers thought for a minute or two and then said at last, 'I'll join you.'

'Good. Let's have another drink. Then you will have to go and see Number One. It is best to do it immediately.'

'Where shall I go? Shall I come here?'

'No, we must not come here again. It is a shame, because it's such a nice place. It is quite comfortable here. Now listen. Tonight, at ten o'clock, walk across Lambeth Bridge. You will see a yellow taxi standing there. The driver will be doing something to the engine. Just say to him, "Is your taxi ready?" and he will say, "It depends on where you want to go." Then you must say, "Take me to Number One, London." He will take you there. You won't be able to see anything because the windows of the taxi will be covered. That is the

rule for the first visit. Later on you will be told where
the place is. That is, when you are one of us.'

'I see.'

'Goodbye and good luck.'

'Goodbye.'

They went out through the doors, each going his own
way.

The secret word is 'Revenge'

In the two years after Rogers joined the organization,
there were some very successful robberies at the houses
of well-known people. A diamond head-dress was
stolen from the Duchess of Denver, and £7,000 worth
of gold and silver disappeared from the house that used
to belong to Lord Peter Wimsey.

One Saturday afternoon in January, Rogers was sitting
in his room when suddenly he heard a noise at the
door. He jumped up, ran quickly through the small hall,
and opened the door. The street was empty. When he
returned, there was an envelope lying on the table. It
was addressed to 'Number Twenty-one.'

He opened it. It said: 'Number Twenty-one — A
special general meeting will be held tonight at the
house of Number One. Be there at 11.30. It will be
dangerous for you to be absent. The secret word is
"Revenge".'

Rogers stood there for a while and thought about the
letter. Then he went to the back of the house. A very
large safe had been built into the house there. He
turned the lock to spell out a secret word, then he
pulled open the heavy metal door, and walked in. It
was like a large room, with a smaller room at the far
end. He opened a drawer marked 'Letters', and put the
piece of paper he had just received into it.

After a few moments he came out and changed the secret word that opened the lock. He then returned to the sitting-room.

'Revenge,' he said. 'Yes — I think so.' He reached for the telephone but then changed his mind. Instead he went upstairs to a very small room under the roof of the house. He crept on his hands and knees into the farthest corner, and there he pressed a hidden spring. This opened a secret door. After crawling through it, he was under the roof of the next house. Here there were three cages. Each cage had a bird in it — a pigeon that could be used to carry messages from one place to another.

He looked carefully out of the little window in the roof. There was nothing in sight, and no one could see him from any other window. On a small piece of thin paper he wrote something in code. He took one of the birds out of its cage and fastened the message to a ring around its leg. Carefully he lifted the bird to the window and it flew away. He saw it disappear into the distance. He looked at his watch and went downstairs again. An hour later he sent off the second bird. Another hour later he sent off the third bird. Then he sat down to wait.

At half-past nine he went upstairs again. It was already dark, but a few stars were shining, and the cold air blew through the open window. He could see something pale on the floor. He picked it up — it was warm and had feathers. The pigeon had brought the answer. Before he read it, he fed the pigeon and put it into one of the cages. He did not lock the little door. 'There is no need for you to die if anything happens to me,' he said to the pigeon.

He left the window open and went downstairs again. The message he had received only had two letters on it, 'O.K.' Everything was all right. He smiled and threw the paper into the fire. He went to his desk and took a gun from a locked drawer. He loaded it and put it into his pocket. Then he sat down to wait again.

At a quarter to eleven he got up and went out. He walked quickly and kept away from the wall, until he came to a well-lit street. Here he took a bus, and he sat in a seat from where he could see everyone who got on or off the bus. After changing buses several times, he came to Hampstead, a very respectable district. He had to cross some open land with a few trees here and there. He saw some other people coming in the same direction. He stopped behind a tree and put on a mask. At the bottom of the mask one could see a white number '21'.

Very soon he came to a house. There were no other houses near it. There was a light in one of the windows. He could see other masked people going there. Altogether he counted six others. The first man knocked and the door was opened a little. There was some whispering and the man was let in. When Rogers came to the door, he knocked three times loudly and twice very gently. When the door was opened, he whispered 'Revenge', and he was let in.

Rogers meets Number One

Number Twenty-one then entered a small room on the left, which was furnished like an office. At the desk sat a large man in evening dress, with a large book in front of him. The door closed behind Rogers and locked. He went to the desk and said, 'Number Twenty-one, sir,' and waited respectfully. The big man looked up. On his black mask Rogers saw the number '1'.

Number One's hard blue eyes looked at Rogers. He made a sign for Rogers to take off his mask. After making sure who he was, Number One said, 'Very well, Number Twenty-one,' and made a mark in his book. His voice was as hard as his eyes. The long look the man gave him seemed to make Rogers uncomfortable. He lowered his eyes and moved his feet. Number One made a sign and Rogers put his mask back on. Then he went out as the next man was coming in.

The Society met in a large room in the house. It was furnished like any other house of this sort. It was brightly lit. Music was playing, and one or two couples were dancing. In one corner there was a bar. A masked man was standing behind the bar, and Rogers asked him for a large whisky. He drank it slowly as the room began to fill with people.

Suddenly it went very quiet. Everyone stopped talking. Rogers looked around. Number One had come in.

'Ladies and gentlemen,' said Number One, 'Two people are missing tonight.' The masks moved. Eyes were turned, counting. 'I am sure you have all heard that we failed to get the plans of the new aeroplane. But you probably do not yet know that our brave friends, Number Sixteen and Number Forty-eight, have been caught by the police.'

There was some angry whispering among the people in the room. 'Some of you may think that our friends will tell the police about us. You have no reason to be afraid of that. The usual orders have been sent out. I have received a report tonight that they will not speak. They will not speak to anyone, ever again. You will be glad to know that these two men will not have to go to prison, where they might decide to talk after a few years.'

The room was quite silent.

'Their families will be cared for, as usual,' Number One continued. 'Numbers Twelve and Thirty-four will take care of this. Please come to the office after the meeting for your orders.'

The two men raised their hands to show that they had understood. 'Ladies and gentlemen, please continue the next dance.'

The music started again. Rogers danced with a girl in a red dress who was standing near him.

'What has happened?' the girl whispered. 'I'm frightened, aren't you? I feel something awful is going to happen tonight.'

'The President does things rather suddenly,' agreed Rogers, 'but it is the safest way.'

'Those poor men —'

A man touched Rogers on the shoulder.

'No talking, please,' he said. The girl trembled.

'We have a traitor'

The music stopped again. The dancers gathered near the President's seat at the end of the room.

'Ladies and gentlemen. You may wonder why this special meeting was called. There is a serious reason. We failed to get the plans of the new aeroplane, because we have a traitor among us. He is here, in this room, now.'

Everyone moved away from those near him. No one seemed to trust the next person.

'You will remember the disappointment we had with the Dinglewood robbery and some others. We have discovered the reason. I am happy to say that we no longer have to worry. The traitor has been found. He will be punished. There will be no more mistakes. The foolish member who introduced this traitor will be taken care of, too. He will not be able to do any more harm to us. There is no cause for fear. Please go on with the next dance.'

When it was finished Number One continued, 'Ladies and gentlemen. I will now name the members who are responsible. Number Thirty-seven!'

A man jumped up with a cry.

'Silence!'

'I never — honestly, I never — I'm innocent.'

'Silence! You have failed because you were not careful. If you have anything to say you may speak later. Sit down.'

Number Thirty-seven sat down in his chair. He wiped his face under the mask with a handkerchief. Two tall men went close to him. The others all moved away as though he had a terrible disease.

'Ladies and gentlemen. I will now name the traitor. Number Twenty-one, stand forward.'

Rogers stepped forward. Forty-eight pairs of eyes seemed to burn through him. They were filled with hate and fear. The unhappy Jukes cried out again.

'Oh, my God! Oh, my God!'

'Silence! Number Twenty-one, take off your mask.'

Rogers pulled the mask from his face. The eyes of the others seemed to eat him.

'Number Thirty-seven, this man was introduced here by you under the name of Rogers. You told us he had been a servant with the Duchess of Denver. You said he had been dismissed for stealing. Did you get any proof of this?'

'I did — I did! I asked other people about him very carefully. I am sure the story was true.'

'Ladies and gentlemen, please continue with the dance.'

Number Twenty-one had his arms twisted behind him and tied up. He stood perfectly still while the others danced. At the end the President spoke again.

Wimsey did not die

'Number Twenty-one, is "Rogers" your true name?'

20 'No.'

'What is your name?'

'Peter Wimsey.'

'We all thought you were dead.'

'That is what I wanted you to think.'

25 'What happened to the real Rogers?'

'He died, somewhere in Africa. I took his place. I became Rogers. Even when I was alone, I walked like Rogers. I ate like Rogers. I read his books and I wore his clothes. In the end I almost thought Rogers'
30 thoughts.'

'I see. The robbery of your own house was arranged?'

'Of course.'

'The robbery of your mother, the Duchess of Denver, was also arranged?'

'It was. The jewels that were stolen were very ugly. No one with good taste would miss them.'

'Numbers Fifteen, Twenty-two, and Forty-nine. You have been watching the prisoner for the past two months. Has he tried to talk to anyone or to send any messages?'

'No,' answered Number Twenty-two. 'We have opened all his letters and listened to his telephone calls. We have also followed him everywhere.'

'Prisoner, have you been alone in this? Speak the truth or the results will be very unpleasant for you.'

'I have been alone. I have not taken any unnecessary risks.'

'It may be so. However, we shall have to silence the prisoner's servant, Bunter. Perhaps also his mother and sister.'

At this the prisoner became excited for the first time. 'Sir, I assure you that my mother and sister do not know anything that could be dangerous to the Society.'

'You should have thought of that before. Ladies and gentlemen, the next dance —'

'No! No!' the others shouted out. They did not wish to wait any longer. 'Finish with him. Get it done. Let us finish the meeting. It is dangerous. The police —'

'Silence!'

The President looked at the crowd. They looked very angry, and he gave in.

'Very well. Take the prisoner away and keep him silent. He will get Number Four treatment. Be sure to explain it to him first.'

'Ah!' came from many lips. Eyes shone cruelly. Strong arms raised Wimsey.

'One moment!' he cried. 'Please let me die quickly.'

'You should have thought about that earlier. Ladies and gentlemen. You can be sure that he will not die quickly.'

5   'Stop! Wait!' cried Wimsey. 'I have something to say. I don't ask for my life — only for a quick death. I — I have something to sell.'

'We don't deal with traitors.'

'But listen. Do you think that I am so stupid that I
10 did not think of this? I have left a letter.'

'A letter? To whom?'

'To the police. If I do not return tomorrow, the letter will be opened.'

'Sir,' interrupted Number Fifteen, 'he has not sent any
15 letters. We have watched him carefully for months.'

'I left the letter with the police before I came to Lambeth.'

'But that was over two years ago. It cannot contain anything of value.'

20 'Oh yes it does. It contains the secret word for the lock on my safe.'

'Has the safe been searched?' asked the President.

'Yes, sir. It contained nothing of importance,' answered Number Fifteen. 'A plan of our organization
25 and the name of this house — nothing important. It can all be changed or hidden before the police find it.'

The inner room

Wimsey smiled and said, 'Did you examine the inner room of the safe?'

30 Number Fifteen was silent.

'You heard what he said. Did you find the inner part?' shouted the President.

'There was no inner part. He is trying to fool us.'

'I am sorry but you are not speaking the truth,' said Wimsey. He was trying to use his ordinary pleasant voice.

'And what is in this inner room of your safe?' asked the President.

'There is a large book containing the names of every member of this Society. I also have their addresses, photographs and fingerprints.'

Everyone was very frightened now.

'Can you prove this?' asked Number One.

'Certainly I can prove this. The name of Number Fifty, for example —'

'Stop! If you mention names, you will certainly get no mercy. There is a fifth treatment. It is especially for people who mention names. Bring the prisoner into my office. Keep the dance going.'

In the office, the President pulled out a gun and faced his prisoner across the desk.

'Now speak!' he said.

'If I were you, I would put that thing away. It would be much better to die that way than to suffer one of your "treatments". I might even do something to make you shoot me.'

'You are very clever, maybe too clever. Now tell me what you know, quickly.'

'Certainly. Tell me when you have heard enough.'

He then leaned forward and began to speak. From the next room came the sound of people dancing. People passing on the street thought there was a party in the house.

A quick death

'Well,' asked Wimsey, 'have you heard enough?'

The President seemed to be smiling under his mask.

He said, 'My Lord, I am very sorry that you are not a member of our Society. Cleverness, hard work, and courage are very valuable to us. Can I talk you into joining? No, I thought not.'

5   He touched a bell on his desk.

'Ask the members to go to the supper-room, please,' he said to the masked man who came in.

The supper-room was on the ground floor. The windows all had heavy curtains on them. They were
10   completely covered. In the centre was a long table with chairs around it. This was the first time that Wimsey had seen the room. At the far end there was an opening in the floor which was the secret way down to some rooms below.

15   The President sat at the head of the table. 'Ladies and gentlemen,' he began, 'I will not hide from you the seriousness of the situation. The prisoner has told me more than twenty names and addresses which we thought were secret. Only their owners and I were supposed to know them. We have been very careless and this will have to be examined.' His voice sounded very angry now. 'The prisoner has also obtained fingerprints and has shown me photographs of them. I also want to know why the inner part of the prisoner's safe was not found.'

'Don't blame them,' said Wimsey, 'I had the door made so that no one could see it.'

'The prisoner has said that the book with the names and addresses is in the inner safe. I believe he is telling the truth. He will tell us the

secret word that opens the safe door in exchange for a
quick death. I think we should accept the offer. What
do you think, ladies and gentlemen?'

'We already know the secret word that will open the
lock,' said Number Fifteen.   5

'Fool! This man has proved to us that he is Lord Peter
Wimsey. Do you think he has forgotten to change the
secret word that unlocks the safe? And then there is the
inner door that you did not see. If he disappears tonight
and the police enter his house — '   10

'I think we should do what the prisoner asks. We
should act quickly; there is not much time,' said one of
the women.

The rest of the crowd seemed to agree with her.

'You hear,' the President said to Wimsey.   15

'And you will keep your promise?'

'We will.'

'Thank you. What about my mother and sister?'

'You are a man of honour. If you can promise that they
know nothing that can harm us, we will not harm them.'   20

'They know nothing.'

'Very well. It is agreed.'

This time it took a little while for the others to agree
but finally all of them did.

'Then I will tell you the secret word. It is "Uselessness. "'   25

'And the inner door?'

'I left it open for the police. I thought that they might
have some trouble finding it.'

'Good. Take the prisoner down into the cellar.
Numbers Twelve and Forty-six will go to Number   30
Twenty-one's house to —'

'No, no!' There were angry shouts from the crowd.
A tall man spoke, 'Why should two more people be
allowed to see the book? We have found one traitor
among us. We have also discovered more than one fool.   35

How do we know that Numbers Twelve and Forty-six are not fools or traitors, too?'

The two men turned to the man who spoke. They were angry. Then a girl's voice interrupted. It was high and trembling.

'I say he is right. We don't want somebody else reading our names. He might tell all of it to the police.'

Another man said, 'I agree. We should not trust anyone.'

The President raised and lowered his shoulders. 'What should we do then?' he asked.

After a moment's silence the girl spoke again. 'I think the President himself should go. He is the only one who knows all the names. Why should we take all the risks while he sits at home and gets rich? Let him go himself, I say.'

There were cries of agreement at this.

The President looked around him and then asked, 'The meeting wishes me to go, then?'

Forty-five hands were raised in agreement. Only the woman who was Number Two did not agree. She remained still and fiercely held on to the arms of her chair.

'Don't go,' she said faintly.

'What Number Two says is of no importance,' said a tall man, rudely. 'Our own ladies would not like it either if they were in the same special position as Number Two.'

Some of the others agreed loudly. Number Two tried to give reasons why the President should not go, but no one was listening.

'The lady seems to be in a special position,' Wimsey said with a smile. 'She probably knows all the names already and there will be nothing new for her in the book. Perhaps she should go herself?'

'I say she must not go,' answered the President. 'I will go. Give me the keys to the house.' One of the men took them out of Wimsey's pocket and gave them to him.

'Are the police watching your house?'   5

'No.'

'Is that the truth?'

'It is the truth.'

At the door the President turned round. 'If I have not returned in two hours, do your best to save yourselves.   10 Number Two will give orders in my absence.'

After he left Number Two rose and said, 'Ladies and gentlemen, supper is over. Start the dancing again.'

The long wait

Down in the cellar, time passed very slowly for Wimsey.   15 He was tired of looking at the instruments used in treatment Number five. Poor Jukes had cried at first but now he just sat there quietly. The four men who guarded them whispered from time to time.

'He has been gone an hour and a half,' one of them said.

Not long afterwards, the door above was opened. 'Bring him up!' cried a voice. Wimsey rose immediately. His face was very pale now.

The members were again sitting around the supper table. Number Two was in the President's chair. She looked at Wimsey like a hungry beast. But she controlled herself before speaking.

5 'The President has been gone for over two hours. What has happened to him?' she asked.

'How should I know?' replied Wimsey. 'Perhaps he took care of himself and left while he could.'

She jumped up angrily and came close to him.

10 'Beast. You are lying!' she said and hit him on the face. 'He would never do that. He is faithful to his friends. What have you done with him? Speak, or I will make you speak. You shall speak.'

'I can only guess, madam. I will not be able to guess
15 any better if you hurt me. Be calm and I will tell you. I think, indeed I fear, that the President must have let the inner door of the safe close behind him. He must have been in such a hurry to look at all the things in the safe that he never noticed the door closing. In that
20 case —'

He looked innocently up at the ceiling.

'What do you mean?'

Wimsey looked around at the others.

'I think I had better begin by describing how my
25 safe works. It was my own idea. The word I gave you is quite correct. But it only opens the door to the first room. The inner room, however, has two doors. One is made of steel. It is painted to look just like the back wall of the outer room. It fits very closely and it is in
30 the same line as the wall of the room. If you measured the outside and the inside of the safe there would be no difference. No one would ever guess that there was another room. This door opens to the main room. I did leave this door open as I told the
35 President.'

'Do you think that the President is so foolish that he would be caught in a simple trap like that? He would put something in the way to keep the door from closing. Then he would go into the room.'

'I am sure he would, madam. The purpose of this door is to make someone think that it is the only one. But hidden behind that one is another one, a sliding door. It is set so carefully into the wall that you would never see it unless you knew it was there. This door was also left open. Our Number One only had to walk through the open door into the inner room. He thought he was going through one door, but in fact he was going through two. I hope I make myself clear?'

'Yes, yes — go on. Make your story short.'

Wimsey bowed and went on slowly.

'The book in which the names are written down is a big one. It lies on a steel shelf at the back of the room. This shelf is about six feet high, three feet wide, and three feet deep. The President is a tall man, and he could read the book on the shelf, but he might find it uncomfortable standing all the time.'

'My God! Go on with your story!'

'You have tied me too tightly,' complained Wimsey.

'I'll have you tied so tightly that your bones will lock together. Beat him! He is trying to waste time.'

'If you beat me I shall not speak at all. Control yourself, madam. Don't forget the President is in danger.'

'Go on!' she cried and stamped her foot in anger.

The President is trapped

'I forgot to say that the inner room has no window of any kind. Well, the steel shelf on which the book lies is balanced on a very fine spring. When the book is

lifted from the shelf, it
rises just a little. This
presses a small electric
switch. Imagine it for
5　yourself. The President
steps into the room, makes
sure the door will stay open
and goes to the shelf. He
quickly takes the book from
10　the shelf to make sure that it is
the right one. He examines a few
pages. He reads a few names, looks
at some photographs and fingerprints.
Meanwhile, silently, but very, very
15　quickly, the door shuts behind him.
He is caught, like an animal in a trap.

'My God! Oh, my God!'

Her hands went up to her face as though she was
going to tear off the mask.

20　'You — you devil! What is the word that opens the
inner door? Quick! I will have it torn out of you — the
word!'

'It is not a hard word to remember although it has
been forgotten before. Do you remember a story you
25　heard when you were a child, *Ali Baba and the Forty
Thieves?* When I had the door made I thought of that
story. The words that open the door are: "Open
Sesame".'

'Ah! And you say there is no window. So no air can
30　get into the room. How long can a man live in that trap
of yours?'

'Oh,' said Wimsey cheerfully, 'I think he might live
for a few hours, but only if he did not waste his strength
and air by shouting and hammering. If we went there
35　at once we should find that he is very well.'

'I shall go myself. Take this man and do what you want with him. But don't kill him till I come back. I want to see him die.'

'One moment,' said Wimsey, not disturbed by what she said. 'You will have to take me with you.'   5

'But why?'

'Because, you see, I'm the only person who can open the door.'

'But you have given me the word. Was that a lie?'

'No, the word is correct. But this door is an electric   10
door, and it opens only when I say the words.'

'When you say them? I will kill you with my own hands. What do you mean, only when you say them?'

'Just what I said. Don't press my throat like that, or the door won't recognize my voice. It wouldn't open   15
for a week once when I had a bad cold. I couldn't speak with my ordinary voice!'

She turned and asked a short, fat man if such a thing was possible.

'Perfectly possible. I'm an electrical engineer. It works   20
a bit like a telephone. The sound is changed into electric waves. They control a needle. When the needle makes the correct movements, the electrical current flows again and opens the door.'

'Couldn't we open it with tools?'   25

'In time we could, but by then — '

She put her hands to her head.

'Wait!' she cried suddenly: 'Somebody must know how to open it. The people who made the thing must know.'   30

'They are in Germany,' said Wimsey.

There was silence. In the distance one could hear the sounds of a new day beginning.

'I give in,' she said at last. 'We must let him go. Take the ropes off him.' She then turned to Wimsey. 'You   35 will set him free?' she asked. 'You are not that much of a devil. Go and save him. I beg you.'

But one of the men cried, 'He is not going anywhere. We will not let him go to the police. The President is finished, that's all. We must try to escape while we can. Throw this fellow in the cellar and tie him up. You, Number Thirty, you know where the switches are, and you know what to do. Give us a quarter of an hour to get away. We will destroy the President's book of names first.'

'No, you can't go. You can't leave him to die. He's your President — your leader — my — I won't let it happen. Set the devil free. One of you help me with the ropes.'

'Stop that now,' one of the men said. He held her wrists while she fought to free Wimsey.

'The police will be here soon,' said another man. 'Come on.'

Number Two suddenly became quiet. 'Yes, you are right. We must not put everyone in danger for one man. Put him in the cellar. Everyone must go to his own place while there is still time.'

'The house will blow up'

Wimsey was pushed into the cellar and left there. At first he was surprised about this. He could understand that they would not let him go even to save Number One. But he could not understand that they would leave him alive. He would tell the police everything. It seemed unbelievable.

'I say,' he cried as the people were leaving. 'It is dark here. Leave the lights on.'

'You won't be in the dark for long. They have set the time switch. The house will blow up in ten minutes.'

So that was it. He was to be blown up with the house. In that case, the President would certainly be dead before the police went to his house. This worried Wimsey. He very much wanted to see the President brought to trial. After all, the police had been waiting   5
six years to catch this society of criminals.

He waited. A few minutes after everyone had gone, he heard someone coming quietly into the cellar.

'Quiet,' a voice said into his ear. Soft hands touched his arms and untied him.   10

'Quick! Quick! They have set the time switch. Follow me as fast as you can. I came back. I said I had left my jewels behind. He must be saved and only you can do it. Quickly!' Wimsey went after her. His arms still hurt from the ropes. She threw open a window.   15

'Now go! Get him out of the safe! Do you promise?'

'I promise.'

'Go, quickly! The time is almost up.'

He took her arm and they ran across the garden. An electric torch was suddenly switched on.

'Is that you, Inspector Parker?' cried Wimsey. 'Get away quickly! The house will blow up any minute.'

Suddenly the garden was full of shouting, hurrying men. Wimsey came to a wall. He pulled himself up, and the woman followed him. They jumped. Everyone was jumping. Then, with a flash and a roar, the house blew up.

Wimsey picked himself up. A cheerful voice called his name out.

'Here I am,' he replied. The next moment he was talking to his friend, Inspector Parker.

5   'Half a dozen of them got blown up with the house,' he said. 'We got the rest. You're a nice fellow. For two years you let us think you were dead. Did anybody know besides Bunter?'

'Only my mother and sister.'

10   'Is he safe?' someone asked.

Wimsey jumped at the cry. The woman was lying on the ground near him.

'Good heavens!' he said. 'I forgot the gentleman in the safe. I want a car, quickly. I have the chief of the
15   whole Society in my safe. He is quietly dying there. Take the woman. I promised we would get there and save him — if we could. He can't last much longer locked up there. He is the man you have wanted for years.'

20   The cold morning had turned the streets grey when they arrived in Lambeth. Wimsey took the woman by the arm, and helped her out of the car. The mask was off now and her face was pale. She was terribly afraid.

Wimsey led them to the back room. The outer door
25   and the steel door were both held open by chairs. The inner door faced them like a plain green wall. 'Open Sesame! Hurry up! Open Sesame!'

Suddenly the green door slid open. The woman jumped forward and caught the body that rolled
30   through into the main room. Number One's clothes were torn and his hands were covered with blood.

Wimsey bent down and felt the man's heart.

'He's all right,' he said. 'He'll live — to go on trial.'

SOLVED BY CHANCE

A new kind of chocolate

Afterwards, Roger Sheringham often thought about the Poisoned Chocolates Case. That was what the newspapers called it. It was perhaps the most perfectly planned murder he had ever known. In the end, the reason for the murder was so easy to understand. But no one had known what it was, at the beginning. The method was interesting, too, once it was known. However, that was not known at first, either. One could see later that here and there, the murderer might have been just a little more careful, but except for some bad luck, the crime would have been a mystery for ever. The murderer had not been prepared for this bad luck.

These are the facts of the case. Chief Inspector Moresby told Sheringham about it one evening, about a week after it had happened.

On Friday morning, 15th November, Sir William Anstruther walked to his club in Piccadilly. He went to the club every morning at ten thirty. He asked if there was any post for him. The doorman gave him three letters and a small parcel. Sir William walked over to the fireplace in the big hall to open them.

A few minutes later Mr Graham Beresford, another member of the club, entered. There were two or three letters for him, and he also went to the fireplace to read them. He smiled at Sir William. The two men knew each other, but they hardly ever spoke.

After looking through his letters, Sir William opened the parcel. A moment later he growled angrily.

Beresford looked at him, and Sir William showed him the letter that was in the parcel.

5 Beresford read the letter and smiled secretly to himself. The letter was from Mason & Sons, makers of fine

10 chocolates. It said that they were producing a new kind of chocolate for men. These chocolates had a special kind of filling. Would

15 Sir William accept them and tell the Company what he thought of them?

'Do they think I'm a girl?' cried Sir William. 'I will tell them what I think of their chocolates. I shall complain

20 to the club about it. This sort of thing can't be allowed here.'

'Well, it's rather lucky for me!' said Beresford. 'It has made me remember something. My wife and I were at the Imperial Theatre last night. We went to see a play

25 about a murder. I said I would give her a box of chocolates, if she could guess who the murderer was before the play was half finished. She did guess, so now I have to buy her a box of chocolates. Have you seen the play? It's quite good.'

30 ## An unfortunate present

Sir William had not seen it and said so. Then he added: 'You want a box of chocolates, you say? Well, take this one. I don't want it'.

For a moment Beresford refused politely. Then, unfortunately for himself, he took it. He said, later, that he did not care about the money he saved, for he was a rich man. But he knew it would take time to go and buy a box of chocolates, and he was very busy that morning.

Luckily, neither the letter nor the paper in which the box was wrapped were thrown into the fire. Beresford just dropped everything on the floor. This was very unusual because both men had thrown the other envelopes in the fire. The servant later picked everything up and put it into the waste-basket. The police found these things there.

Of the three people involved in the events leading to the murder, Sir William was the most noticeable one. He was just under fifty and had a bright red face. He was rather fat, and looked like the old sort of country gentleman. His manners and his language were rather rough, but women liked him, and he had many women friends.

Compared with him, Beresford was a very ordinary man. He was tall, dark and rather good-looking. He did not talk much. His father had left him a lot of money. But he did not like being idle, and he owned several companies in which he took an interest.

Beresford was born with money and he continued to earn it. It was, therefore, not surprising that he should marry someone rich. His wife, Mrs Beresford, was the third person in this case.

Mrs Beresford was the daughter of a wealthy businessman in Liverpool. She had about half a million pounds. Beresford's friends all said that he would have married her even if she had had no money. She was a tall, serious-minded woman with a good education. She seemed the ideal wife for him. She had some very strict ideas, but this did not trouble Beresford. He was quite ready to be strict also. As far as anyone knew, the Beresfords were a very happily married couple.

Beresford gave her the box of chocolates just after lunch. They were having coffee and she opened them immediately. Beresford did not believe in spoiling good coffee with sweets, and he refused the first one. She ate it, and at once complained that the filling was very strong. It seemed to burn her mouth.

Beresford told her that these were a new kind, that one could not buy in the shops yet. He was curious and also ate one. He also noticed a burning taste. It was not too strong but had an unpleasant taste. There was also a smell rather like a kind of nut, a bitter almond.

'They are certainly strong,' he said, 'they must be filled with pure alcohol.'

'Oh, the makers would not do that, I am sure,' said his wife. Taking another, she continued, 'But I think I rather like them anyway.'

Beresford ate one more. He liked it even less than the first. 'I don't like them at all. They take all the feeling out of my tongue. You shouldn't eat any more. I think there is something wrong with them.'

'Well, I suppose they are trying to make something new. But they do burn. I'm not sure now whether I like them or not.

Beresford is ill

A few minutes later, Beresford left. He had to go to a business meeting. His wife was still eating the chocolates, trying to decide if she liked them or not. Beresford remembered this conversation with her very clearly later on. It was the last time he saw her alive.

He left
home at about half-
past two. At a quarter to four he
arrived at his club. He had come in
a taxi and was almost unconscious. The driver and the   5
doorman helped him into the building. Both later said
that he was extremely pale, and looked directly in front
of him. His lips were blue and his skin felt very cold.
He could think clearly, however. When they had taken
him up the stairs, he was able to walk into the hall with   10
the help of the doorman.

The doorman was very much afraid and wanted to
call a doctor right away. But Beresford did not want to
cause any trouble and would not let him. He said that
there was something wrong with his stomach, and he   15
would be better again soon.

After the doorman had gone, he added to Sir William
Anstruther, 'I believe it was those chocolates you gave
me. When I tasted them I thought there was something

wrong with them. I had better go and find out about
my wife.' Suddenly he stopped. His body became stiff
and his jaws would not open. His blue lips were twisted
into a terrible smile. He held the arms of the chair
5 tightly. Sir William was frightened, and he noticed a
smell of bitter almonds.

He thought the man was dying and he called for the
doorman and a doctor. The other members of the club
helped to move the body to a more comfortable place.
10 Before the doctor arrived there was a telephone
message from a frightened servant. He wanted
to know if Beresford was there, as
Mrs Beresford was very ill.
Actually she was already dead.
15 Beresford did not die. He
had eaten less of the
poison than his wife who
must have eaten at least
three more chocolates
20 after he left her. The
poison did not act so
quickly in Beresford and
the doctor had time to
save him. In fact, it
25 became clear later on that
he had not taken enough to
kill him. By eight o'clock that
night he was conscious again.
The next day he was much better.

30   **Murder!**

Poor Mrs Beresford was not so lucky. The doctor
arrived too late to save her. She died very quickly while
she was still unconscious.

It was reported to the police that Mrs Beresford had died from poison. This brought them into the matter. The police soon realized that the poison had been in the chocolates.

Sir William was questioned and the police found the letter and the paper which had been around the parcel. Before Beresford was out of danger, an officer had gone to Mason & Sons. Police detectives in London move quickly.

At first the police thought there had been a mistake made at Mason & Sons. They thought that perhaps some worker had put too much oil of bitter almonds into the filling mixture for the chocolates. However, the manager told them that the company never used oil of bitter almonds. He read the letter with the greatest care. He said that it was a forgery. His company had sent neither the letter nor the chocolates. They had not even thought of producing a new kind of chocolate. The ones in the box looked just like their ordinary kind.

The manager took the paper off one of the chocolates and examined it closely. He then pointed to a mark on the underside of the chocolate. There was a small hole. Through this hole the original filling was removed, and the poison was introduced. It would have been quite simple to close the hole with a piece of soft chocolate. The police inspector looked at the chocolates carefully and agreed with the manager. It was clear that someone had tried to murder Sir William Anstruther.

The detectives now worked harder than ever. The chocolates were sent to scientists to be carefully examined. Both Sir William and Beresford were questioned again by the police, but neither of them could help much.

Sir William could not think of anyone who would want to kill him. He no longer lived with his wife,

whose home was in the south of France. He had no
children. Also he was not a rich man: there was no land
or property for anyone to receive on his death. If
Sir William died, no one would gain anything.

5   The examination of the chocolates told the police two
things. Oil of bitter almonds had not been used as the
poison. Nitrobenzene, a substance with a similar smell,
had been used. This is normally used in the
manufacture of colour for cloth, and it was surprising
10   to see it used as a poison. Each chocolate in the top
row contained exactly the same amount of the poison,
mixed with something sweet. All the other rows were
completely harmless.

The police discovered that the paper on which the
15   letter had been written was the kind always used by
Mason's. The company's address was printed on it.
There was, however, no way of knowing how the
murderer had obtained it. The edges of the paper were
rather yellow and the paper must, therefore, have been
20   quite old. The typewriter which had been used could
not be found at Mason's, either. From the wrapping
paper, the police discovered that the parcel had been
posted at the Southampton Street Post Office, between
8.30 and 9.30 on the evening before the murder. The
25   address was printed in large, clear letters.

One thing was clear. The
person who had wanted to
murder Sir William had
not wanted to be
30   caught.

Who wanted to kill Sir William?

'Now you know as much as we do, Mr Sheringham,' said Chief Inspector Moresby as he finished telling the story. 'If you can say who sent the chocolates, you will know a lot more than we do.'   5

'Yes, it's a difficult case,' agreed Sheringham. 'I met a man only yesterday who went to school with Beresford. He tells me that the poor man is very sad because of his wife's death. He is quite ill. I wish you could find out who sent those chocolates, Moresby.'   10

'So do I, Mr Sheringham,' replied Moresby hopelessly.

'It might have been anyone in the whole world,' Sheringham continued. 'What about a woman's jealousy? Sir William's private life does not seem to be very respectable. He is always falling in love with   15
someone new. Maybe one of those he grew tired of ...'

'That's just what I have been enquiring about,' replied Inspector Moresby. 'That was the first thing that came into my mind. The clearest thing about the murder is that it is a woman's work. Only a woman would send   20
poisoned chocolates to a man. Another man would send some poisoned wine, or something like that.'

'That's a good point,' said Roger thoughtfully. 'Couldn't Sir William help you?'

'Couldn't or wouldn't,' Moresby replied, rather   25
annoyed. 'At first I thought he suspected a woman and was protecting her. But now I don't think so.'

Roger did not seem quite so sure. 'I think I remember a case like this before. Didn't some madman send some poisoned chocolates to the Chief of Police himself? A   30
good crime is usually imitated by others, you know.'

Moresby's face grew brighter. 'It is strange you should say that. I was thinking the same thing myself. I have tested every other possibility. As far as I know, nobody

would gain anything from Sir William's death. Nobody
would have a reason to kill him for revenge. That leaves
only the possibility you just mentioned. I have decided
that the chocolates were sent by someone with no sense
5 of responsibility. This person probably did not even
know Sir William. If it was some mad woman, how will
we ever find her?'

'Chance will come to our help,' said Roger. 'Many
cases are solved just by chance, aren't they?'

10 If Moresby had had any hopes that Roger Sheringham
would help him, he was disappointed. Roger agreed
with the Chief Inspector that it was the work of some
mad woman. For this reason he would not agree to
help. It was one of those difficult cases; there would
15 be endless enquiries. A private detective could not do
this sort of work very well. It was best done by the
local police. Still, he thought about it a great deal in the
next few days.

A useful meeting

20 During a chance meeting a week later he became
interested in the case again.

Roger was walking down Bond Street to buy a new
hat, when he saw Mrs Verreker coming towards him.
This lady was very rich, pretty, and a widow. She
25 admired Roger, but he did not like her. The reason was
that she talked, and talked, and talked. He tried to
escape across the road, but there was too much traffic.
He was caught.

'Oh, Mr Sheringham,' she cried. 'You are just the
30 person I want to see. Please tell me, are you taking up
this case of poor Joan Beresford's death?'

Roger smiled politely. He tried to say something, but
Mrs Verreker continued talking:

'I was very sad when I heard about it. You see, Joan
Beresford and I were such very close friends. The worst
thing about the whole story is that Joan was responsible
for her own death. Isn't that terrible?'

Suddenly, Roger did not want to escape any more.   5

'What did you say?' he just managed to ask.

'I suppose it's just bad luck,' Mrs Verreker continued.
'It was sad enough, but this makes it even sadder. You
know about the bet she made with her husband? He
had to give her a box of chocolates. If Beresford had   10
won the bet himself, Sir William would never have
given him the poisoned chocolates, would he, and he
wouldn't have given them to Joan? Well ...' She lowered
her voice to make what she was saying seem more
important. 'I have not told anyone else this, but you   15
will understand. Joan cheated!'

'What do you mean?' Roger asked, very surprised.

Mrs Verreker was pleased with the effect of her
words.

'She had seen the play before. We went together, in   20
the first week it came to the theatre. She knew who the
murderer was in the play all the time. But she did not
say so to her husband.'

Roger whistled. 'That certainly was bad luck,' he said.

'Yes,' Mrs Verreker continued. 'Joan Beresford of all   25
people! I should never have thought she would do a
thing like that. Such a nice girl. She is not very generous
with her money even though she is so very rich. But
that isn't very important. Of course, she only did it in
fun, to play a joke on her husband. But I always thought   30
that Joan was such a serious girl, Mr Sheringham. She
used to speak of truth and honour, and being fair. Often
she would say that this wasn't fair, and that wasn't
honest and so on. Well, she has certainly been punished
for not acting honestly, hasn't she, poor woman? It   35

shows that you can't judge people by what they say. Maybe she wasn't as truthful and honest as she always pretended to be. If she could deceive her husband in such a small matter, well, I don't want to say any more.
5 You understand what I mean, don't you? The way people behave is so interesting. Don't you agree, Mr Sheringham?'

'Yes, sometimes it is very interesting,' replied Roger seriously. 'You mentioned Sir William Anstruther just
10 now. Do you know him?'

'I used to know him. What an unpleasant man he is! He is always chasing after women, but he soon grows tired of them. That's what someone told me, anyway,' she added quickly.

15 'What a pity you were not at the Imperial Theatre with the Beresfords that evening. They wouldn't have made the bet then,' said Roger.

'But I wasn't there, unfortunately. I was at a different theatre.'

20 Roger then had to listen to what Mrs Verreker thought of all the plays in London. However, he did manage to find out that she had photographs of Mrs Beresford and Sir William Anstruther. She was willing to let him go to her house and take them away.

25 As soon as she was out of sight, he called a taxi and went to her place. He thought it would be better to get the pictures immediately. If he went back later, he might have to pay for the pictures with another long conversation.

30 A servant came to the door, and took him up to the sitting-room at once. A corner of the room was filled with pictures of Mrs Verreker's friends. There were many photographs. Roger examined them with interest and finally took six away with him. They were of
35 Sir William, Mrs Beresford, Beresford, two other men

whom he
did not know,
and one of Mrs Verreker
herself. He wanted to be careful,
so that she would not know
exactly what he was interested in.

Roger asks many questions

For the rest of the day he was very busy.

He took a taxi to the Anglo-Eastern Perfumery
Company. There, he asked a lot of questions to obtain   10
information about all the company's branches.

Then he went to Wilson's. This company advised
people on how to save their money. People paid them
a small sum to find out which companies were safe to
invest in, and which ones were not. This was helpful,   15
as many companies were not as good as they seemed
to be. If you invested your money in them, you would
lose it.

Roger telephoned the manager of Mason's, and asked
him where they bought the paper for their letters. He   20
was given the name and address of a well-known shop,
and went there immediately.

Roger told the young woman in the shop that he
wanted some very special writing paper. He gave the
details, and was finally shown a sample book with   25
many different kinds of paper in it. As Roger looked

through the pages, he mentioned that a friend of his had been in the shop about a week earlier, and had said it was very good. By chance he also had a photograph of this friend in his pocket, and he showed it to the young woman. He asked her, 'Do you recognize him?' The woman looked at the picture. She did not seem very interested, but she said that she did recognize the man.

Roger went back to his house to have dinner. Afterwards he went out for a walk and was soon in Piccadilly, near the Imperial Theatre. The play started at half-past eight. It was now twenty-nine minutes past eight. He had to spend the evening somehow, so he went in.

Early the next morning Roger went to see Moresby at his office.

'Moresby,' he said to his friend, 'I want you to do something for me. Can you find for me a taxi driver who took a man from somewhere near Piccadilly to Southampton Street Post Office at about half-past nine the evening before the murder? I am also looking for a driver who took a man the other way. It is possible that only one taxi was used, but I am not sure. Do you think you can do that?'

'What's the idea, Mr Sheringham?' Moresby asked suspiciously.

'I am just trying to destroy a false story,' replied Roger. 'By the way, I also know who sent the chocolates to Sir William. Now I am just collecting all the proof for you. Telephone me when you have found those taxi drivers.'

He left. Moresby was standing there with his mouth open, looking after him.

Roger spent the rest of the day trying to find out something about a typewriter. He went to a number of shops, and said that he wanted to buy a very special sort of typewriter. No other kind would do. At last, Roger found a shop where they had sold one of these typewriters less than a month ago.

A helpful taxi driver

At half-past four he went back to his house, and an hour later he received a telephone call from Moresby. He had been waiting for it.

'I have fourteen taxi drivers here in my office,' he said. 'What do you want me to do with them?'

'Keep them there until I come, Inspector,' replied Roger politely.

The meeting with the taxi drivers did not last long. He showed a photograph to each one in turn. He held the photograph so that Moresby could not see it. The ninth man said he recognized the person in the picture. Then Moresby sent them all away and looked at Roger.

'Mr Sheringham, perhaps you could explain to me what you are doing?'

'Certainly, Inspector. I have been doing your work for you. I have the answer. I have proof here.' He took a letter from his pocket and showed it to Moresby. 'Was that typed on the same machine as the letter from Mason's, or was it not?'

Moresby examined the letter, and then pulled the forgery from his desk drawer. He compared them closely. At last he said with a serious voice, 'Mr Sheringham, where did you get this?'

'In a typewriter shop in the city. The machine was bought by an unknown person a few weeks ago. The people in the shop recognized him from the photograph I have just shown the taxi drivers. The machine was used for a time in the shop to see if it was all right. I was therefore able to get an example of its work.

'And where is the machine now?'

'Oh, at the bottom of the river, I suppose,' Roger smiled. 'I tell you, our murderer does not take any chances, but it doesn't matter. I have the proof here.'

'Yes, that's all right,' agreed Moresby, 'but what about the Mason's writing paper?'

'That was taken from a book of samples. I thought so when I saw the yellow edges. I can prove that the man was in the shop. There is also an empty space in the book, where the sample used to be.'

'Excellent,' said Moresby.

'The taxi driver can prove that what the murderer said is not true. He took the person to Southampton Street and back, between ten past nine and twenty-five past. The parcel must have been posted at about this time.'

Who is the murderer?

'And who is the murderer, Mr Sheringham?'

'It is the person whose photograph is in my pocket,' answered Roger. 'By the way, do you remember what I was saying about chance? Well, that's what happened in this case. By chance I met a silly woman in Bond

Street. She gave me a bit of information which told me who had sent the chocolates. There were other possible murderers but I tested them, and showed that my first idea was right.'

'But who was the murderer, then?' Moresby asked again.

Roger did not answer Moresby; he just went on. 'It was such a beautiful plan. We never understood for a moment what a mistake we had made. It was the mistake the murderer wanted us to make.'

'What was that?'

'Well, he wanted us to think that the murderer's plan had failed. We were to think that the wrong person had been killed. In fact the plan worked very well. The right person was killed.'

Moresby was really surprised at this. 'What do you mean by that?' he asked Roger.

'The murderer had wanted to kill Mrs Beresford. It was a very clever plan. He thought of everything. It was quite natural that Sir William would give the chocolates to Beresford. The murderer also knew that we would look for someone who wanted to kill Sir William. We never thought of looking for someone who might want to kill the dead woman. He also hoped we would imagine that a woman had done it.'

At this point Moresby interrupted Roger, 'Good Heavens! You don't mean to say that Sir William himself …'

'The murderer wanted to kill Mrs Beresford. He liked her enough at the beginning, but all he really wanted was her money. The trouble was that she never gave him any. He needed it very badly. This I am very sure of. He owned several companies. I made a list of them. All of them are doing very badly at the moment. He had lost all his money, and he needed some more.

'We were so puzzled by the nitrobenzene at first, you will remember. That was actually quite simple. One of the companies he owned was a cloth factory, Anglo-Eastern Textiles. That is how he knew that nitrobenzene was poisonous. He probably did not get it from his factory, he is too clever for that. He probably made it himself. It is not very difficult.'

Moresby said, 'But Sir William isn't the sort of man to do this. He is rather rough, but he is a gentleman, and this is such a cruel crime!'

Beresford is the one

'Sir William?' said Roger. 'Who is talking about Sir William? I told you I had the murderer's photograph in my pocket.'

He pulled it out and gave it to Moresby, who was very surprised. 'Beresford is the man,' Roger went on. 'Beresford murdered his wife.'

'But —' said Moresby.

'Yes, Beresford is the man. He didn't like his wife's strict ideas. He liked it even less that she would not give him any of her money. I am sure he married her for her money. When she would not give him any, and he needed it, he planned to kill her. He thought about it very carefully. He took his wife to the Imperial Theatre. Between the first and second acts, he went out. I went there

myself to see what time it must have been. He quickly
went to Southampton Street and posted the parcel. The
taxi driver who drove him there recognized him.
Beresford had ten minutes to do it. It would not matter
if he came back a few minutes late.   5

'The rest was easy. He knew that Sir William came
to the club every morning at ten-thirty. He also knew
that Sir William would get angry about the chocolates,
and give him them to him if he had a good reason. He
mentioned the bet to Sir William. He knew that the   10
police would make many mistakes. He was also careful
not to throw the letter or the wrapping paper into the
fire. This way, it would look to the police as though
some mad person had sent the chocolates to
Sir William.'   15

'That's very clever, Mr Sheringham,' said Moresby
generously. 'What did the lady tell you that gave you
the idea?'

'Well, it wasn't what she told me. It was what I
guessed from her words. She told me that Mrs Beresford 20
knew the answer to that bet. I thought at once that a
very honest woman like Mrs Beresford would never
make a bet if she already knew the answer. Therefore
the truth was that she didn't make such a bet. That
meant that Beresford was lying. It also meant that   25
Beresford wanted those chocolates for some other
reason. After all, Beresford was the only one who told
us about the bet.

'He put the same amount of poison in each chocolate
so that he could eat some. He knew that he could eat   30
two without dying. If he ate some of the chocolates,
who would ever guess that he himself had poisoned
them? It was a very clever idea.'

Moresby rose to his feet and said, 'Well,
Mr Sheringham, I am very grateful to you. So you found 35

all this out by chance, eh? But, you know, there was one thing that Beresford could not have been sure about. It was a very important thing. What if Sir William had given the chocolates to one of his lady friends?'

Roger sighed. 'Really, Moresby! That would not have been so very serious. You don't think that Beresford sent Sir William the poisoned chocolates, do you? Of course not! He sent Sir William a box of harmless ones. He changed it for the box with the poisoned ones on his way home!'

THE STOLEN GOLD BARS

Suppositions

'In our job,' remarked Thorndyke, the private detective, 'we must always be careful not to suppose that we know things. We sometimes make suppositions without even thinking about it. When an ordinary person talks about a case, he nearly always supposes that certain things are very important. He will pay a lot of attention to those things. Other things he supposes are unimportant, and he therefore forgets about them. We must never accept such suppositions. We must look at each fact separately. In this way, what seems unimportant will often become very important.'

Thorndyke was talking after we had heard about a case from a Mr Halethorpe. Halethorpe worked for the Sphinx Insurance Company and his company was working on this case. At the time I did not understand Thorndyke's words. Later on, however, when the case was solved, I did understand them. I realized that I had made the sort of mistake he had warned us about.

'I hope I have not come at a difficult time,' said Mr Halethorpe. 'It is after working hours.'

'My work is also my pleasure,' said Thorndyke. 'You will give me some pleasure and I welcome you. Pull up a chair, and tell us your story.'

Mr Halethorpe laughed. Then he began his story. 'I don't know if you can help us. It is not your usual business to find lost property. I thought I would just tell you about our difficulties. We are in danger of losing about four thousand pounds, and we don't like that. This is what happened.

'About two months ago, the London office of Akropong Gold Mining Company asked us to insure a parcel of gold bars. They were being sent to the big jewellers, Minton and Borwell.

5   'The bars were to be put on a ship in Accra, West Africa, to go to Bellhaven. That is the nearest port to Minton and Borwell's factory. Well, we insured the bars, and the matter was settled. We have done business with the Akropong Company before, so that was no
10   problem. The bars were put on the ship, the *Labadi*, at Accra. Later they were safely landed at Bellhaven and delivered to a man from Minton and Borwell.'

The gold disappears

'So far there was no trouble. Then came the accident.
15   The gold was put on the train at Bellhaven, and sent to Ancaster, where the factory is. The trains do not go directly from Bellhaven to Ancaster. You have to change trains at Garbridge. This is a small country station close to the River Crouch. Here the box was taken out of the
20   train from Bellhaven, and locked in the station-master's office. It had to wait for the train to Ancaster.

'It seems that the station-master was called away and stayed away longer than he had expected. When the train arrived, he hurried back. He was a bit worried by
25   now. However, everything was all right. The box was there and it was put on the train. He gave it to the guard himself. All was well on the rest of the journey. At the station in Ancaster there was a car from the factory. The box was put into the car and taken directly
30   to the factory. It was opened in the private office. But there it was found to be full of lead pipe.'

'I suppose,' said Thorndyke, 'that it was not the original box.' 'No, it wasn't,' replied Halethorpe,

'but it was a very good imitation. The writing and all the marks were correct. It is clear that the exchange was made in the station-master's office. We found out later that although the door was locked, one of the windows was not. The one that faces the garden was not closed properly. There were some footprints just outside this window.'

'What time did this happen?' asked Thorndyke.   10

'The Ancaster train came in at a quarter past seven. By then it was already dark.'

'And what day was it?'

'The day before yesterday.'

'Are you refusing to pay for the loss?'   15

'We don't want to refuse, but we feel that the railway company was not careful enough. We might be able to get the money back from them. Naturally, we would prefer to find the gold again. It can't be far away.'

'I don't know about that,' said Thorndyke. 'This was   20 a carefully planned crime. The false box must have been prepared by someone who knew exactly what it must look like. He must also have known when it would arrive in Bellhaven. We must believe that the thieves thought very carefully about how they were   25 going to take the gold away safely. How far is Garbridge from the river?'

'Less than half a mile across the marshes. Detective Inspector Badger asked the same question. I think you know him. He is working on the case.'

'Of course,' said Thorndyke. 'A heavy box like this would be easier to move by water than by land. It is also easier to hide on a river. The box might have been hidden on a small ship, or even a boat. The bars could even have been hidden separately among other goods. If necessary, they could have been dropped into the water at a marked place. They could be picked up later when the search was over.'

Halethorpe said sadly, 'Do you think we will ever see the gold again?'

'We need not give up hope,' replied Thorndyke. 'But we must realize that it will be difficult. The thieves have the gold now. Gold cannot be destroyed even if it is broken up into very small pieces. But if it were melted down, then it would be impossible to say if it was the same gold.'

'Well, the police are looking after the case now,' said Halethorpe. 'But our company would be very happy if you could help. What do you say?'

'I am willing to try, but I don't know if I can do very much. Could you give me a letter to the shipping company and another to Minton and Borwell?'

'Of course. I'll write to them now. But it seems to me that you are starting your search just where there is nothing to be learnt. The box was stolen after it left the ship and before it reached Minton and Borwell.'

'The point is this,' said Thorndyke, 'the robbery was well planned. The thieves must have had special information. That information must have come either from the ship or the factory. We must, therefore, try to discover where it all started. After that we can try to find the box.'

Halethorpe agreed and then wrote the two letters. He asked the factory and the shipping company to help Thorndyke as much as they could. He wished us good luck and then left.

'Quite an interesting little problem. It is not like our usual ones,' remarked Thorndyke. 'This is really a case for the police. It will need a lot of careful questions, and a lot of thought. Let us try to find out where the crime began.'

'Where are you going to start?' I asked.

'At the beginning, of course,' he replied. 'Tomorrow we will go to Bellhaven and see what we can find there.'

'What do you think you can discover there? We already know the box started from there,' I asked.

'There are a number of different possibilities. The question is whether any of them happened. That is what I must know before I can begin a detailed examination of this case.'

'I don't understand. Would it not be best to start from the scene of the robbery?' I asked. 'Or perhaps you have seen some possibilities that I have not seen.'

The Custom-house at Bellhaven

The next morning we arrived in Bellhaven. Thorndyke said, 'I think we had better go first to the Custom-house. The gold must have been shown to the customs officers there, to see if there was any tax to pay on it. We must be sure that the gold was really in the box when it was delivered to the man from the factory. We know the box was stolen from the station at Garbridge, but it might not have had the gold in it. It is likely that it did, but it has not been proved yet.'

We therefore went to the harbour and found the Custom-house. The officer there was a very friendly man. Thorndyke explained why he had come, and the man was quite willing to help.

5 He explained that there was no tax to pay on gold coming into the country, but it had to be shown to the Customs officers. The only exception was gold going to the Bank of England. The gold for Minton and Borwell was clearly a private box and it was therefore

10 examined. He called to another man in the office, 'Jefferson, show these gentlemen the report on the box of gold bars from the *Labadi.*'

'Would it also be possible to talk to the officer who opened the box?' asked Thorndyke.

15 The first officer agreed. 'Jeffson, let these gentlemen read the report. When they have finished, please take them to the officer who signed it.'

We followed Jeffson to another office where he gave us the report. It described the box very carefully. It was

20 thirteen inches long, twelve inches wide, and nine inches deep. It weighed one hundred and seventeen pounds and three ounces. The gold was in the form of four bars and weighed one hundred and thirteen pounds and two ounces.

25 When we had finished with the report, Thorndyke asked to see the officer who had signed the report. His name was Byrne.

We went to look for him and found him near the dock, looking at a large number of boxes of all kinds.

30 He was carefully examining some of them. When we arrived, he looked at us in an unfriendly way.

'We would like to talk to you about the gold that was on the *Labadi,*' explained Thorndyke. 'Did you weigh the bars separately from the box?'

35 'I did,' replied Mr Byrne.

'Did you weigh each bar separately?'

'I did not.'

'What did the bars look like? I mean, what shape and size were they?'

'I've never had much to do with gold bars,' answered Mr Byrne. 'I suppose they were just ordinary ones. Each one was about nine inches long, four inches wide and two inches deep.'

'How were they placed in the box?'

'The bars were covered with a thick cloth, and were pressed tightly in the box. There was about half an inch all around for the cloth. The box itself was an inch and a half thick. It was strengthened by iron bands.'

'Did you seal the box after you were finished with it?'

'I did. I sealed it very carefully. No one could open that box without breaking the seals first. Everything was done correctly, and then I gave it back to the officer from the ship. I saw him hand it to the man from the company. Everything was in order when it left the dock.'

'Thank you. That is what I wanted to be sure of,' said Thorndyke. He put his notebook into his pocket, and we prepared to leave. He then turned to me and said, 'We've finished with the customs. I am glad we came here first. We learned a great deal here.'

'We know now,' I suggested, 'that the box was all right when it left here. We can start at Garbridge with that useful fact.'

'There is more than that. We must know a few more details. Let us go to see the man who handles the company's business here. We will show him

Halethorpe's letter. It will be good to learn all we can before we go to the scene of the crime.'

'I don't know what else there is to learn. However, I suppose you have some ideas. Let's go there then,' I replied.

The manager of the shipping agent's office looked at us carefully as we came in. He read Halethorpe's letter and then spoke to us. 'You have come about the stolen gold. Well, it wasn't stolen here. You had better go to Garbridge, hadn't you?'

'I know that,' answered Thorndyke. 'But since we are here, we decided to ask some questions first. Who has the ship's papers for the gold?'

'I have a copy of the bill of lading, if that's what you mean. That's the detailed list of what is in the cargo. The captain has the original one.'

'Could I see it?' asked Thorndyke.

The man was not very willing to give it to Thorndyke. Finally, though, he found it and handed it over. Thorndyke copied many details down in his little notebook. Then he asked to see a copy of the ship's cargo list.

'The details on the cargo list are merely copied from the bill of lading.'

'I would like to see it anyway,' Thorndyke said.

The man was impatient now, 'There is nothing on the cargo list that isn't on the bill of lading. I have already told you that.'

'I realize that, but I would still like to see it,' said Thorndyke.

A bag of beans

The man finally went into another room and came back with a set of papers. They were as thick as a book, and he threw them noisily onto the table. 'There you are. The ship's cargo list. This is the part dealing with the gold. The other papers deal with the rest of the cargo. I suppose you are not interested in that.'

But he was mistaken. After finishing with the details of the gold bars, Thorndyke looked carefully at the whole list. The man became very impatient and said in an angry voice, 'If you want to look at the whole thing you must excuse me. I have work to do.'

Still, he did not go away. He was surprised to see Thorndyke copying down so many details. Finally he said, 'Good God, sir! What could a bag of beans have to do with a gold robbery? They are still in the ship, you know.'

'I supposed they were, as they are addressed to London,' Thorndyke said. He continued down the list. There was a bag of seeds, a box of rocks, a box of six inch screws, some African nuts, and many other things. The man became more and more impatient. Thorndyke paid no attention to him, and continued copying all the things he wanted. He took all the details of some of the things, such as size and weight. I could not understand it either.

At last he finished. He closed and put away his notebook. The manager was pleased and sighed with relief. 'Is there anything else, sir?' he asked. 'I suppose you want to look at the ship too?' He was sorry he had said that for Thorndyke asked him, 'Is the ship still here?'

'Yes, they will finish unloading at twelve,' he replied. 'Then the ship will sail for London. It will arrive there tomorrow morning.'

'I don't think I need to look at the ship,' Thorndyke thanked him and then we left to go to the station.

'Well,' I said, 'you have certainly collected a lot of

information. I just cannot see what it has to do with our problem.'

Thorndyke looked at me. 'Jervis! You surprise me. My dear fellow, it is as clear as daylight.'

5   'What do you mean by "it"?' I asked, rather annoyed.

'I mean we have the important facts from which we can find out how the robbery was done. When we are on the train you must look at my notes. I am sure you will find them interesting.'

10   'I doubt it,' I said, 'but meanwhile we are wasting a lot of time. Halethorpe does not want to know how the gold was stolen. He just wants it back.'

'That is true, indeed. You are showing good common sense. All the same, I think it will be useful to know
15   all we can about the method of robbery. I agree with you that we have spent enough time just finding facts. The important thing now is to continue at Garbridge. But I see our train is coming. Let us hurry.'

The journey to Garbridge

20   When we were on the train, Thorndyke handed me his notebook and I studied it carefully. I was very puzzled, and he looked at me with a smile on his face. I read through the notes again and again but I still could not understand it. I could not see what African nuts, screws,
25   and seeds had to do with the robbery. After a while, I closed the book angrily and gave it back to Thorndyke.

'It's no use,' I said to him, 'I can't see any meaning in it.'

'It doesn't matter. The most important work is still
30   before us. It may prove to be quite difficult. We must get those gold bars back if it is at all possible. Well, here we are at Garbridge. Oh, I see an old friend of ours is here.'

As the train came in to the station, I looked out. Yes, there was someone waiting there. It was Inspector Badger of the London Police Force.

'We really don't need him, do we?' I remarked.

'No, we don't,' agreed Thorndyke, 'but we shall have 5 to work with him. After all, this is his case. How do you do, Inspector?' he said as we met Badger. He had hurried toward us, and he was very happy to see us.

'I thought you might be here. We heard that Halethorpe asked your advice. But this isn't the London 10 train.'

'No,' said Thorndyke, 'we have just come from Bellhaven. We wanted to be sure the gold was in the box when it started there.'

'I could have told you that two days ago,' said 15 Badger. 'We asked the Customs people right away. That was easy, but the rest of the case isn't.'

'You have no idea how the box was taken from the station?' asked Thorndyke.

'Oh, yes, that is quite clear. It was lifted out through 20 the window in the station-master's office. The other one was lifted into the office in the same way. That night, two men were seen carrying a heavy parcel towards the marshes. It was about the same size as the box. But that is all we know. The gold seems to have 25 disappeared completely. We are still looking for it, of course. I am staying here with two of my men. I am sure that it is still somewhere around here. I hope to catch someone trying to move it.'

A perfect place for a robbery   30

As the Inspector was talking, we walked towards the river. We stopped on the bridge leading to the village on the opposite side. Thorndyke looked down the river and over the marsh beside it.

'A perfect place for a robbery,' he said. 'The river is so near the sea, and there are so many little streams around here. It would be very easy to hide the gold for a while and pick it up later. Have you seen any strange boats around here lately?'

'Yes. There is a small dirty-looking sailing boat from Leigh. The two men who came with it are not from here, that's quite certain. They don't know the river and their boat is stuck on the mud. There it is now, over on the mud on the far side. But I am sure the gold is not on that boat. I have looked over every inch of it.'

'What about that barge over there?'

'That is there quite often. The captain and his son are very respectable people. They live here. Look, you can see them now, in the small rowing boat. They are going out to the barge now. They are probably going to leave tonight. But wait a minute ...'

The Inspector stared hard at the river. Then he became quite excited. 'I don't think they are going to their barge. It seems to me that they are going to the sailing boat on the mud.'

The Inspector took out his binoculars and watched the two men. Two old fishermen, who were walking across the bridge, stopped to watch, too.

One of the men in the small rowing boat gave a shout, and two men came out of the sailing boat. Then they got into the little boat, and all four went to the barge.

'It looks as if those fellows are going onto the barge,' said one of the fishermen.

'Then they will have to work,' said the other.

The two men from the sailing boat began to lift up the anchor. Meanwhile, the captain and his son got the sails ready.

Badger was still looking at the barge. 'It seems strange,' he said, 'they haven't taken anything on board with them.'

'Have you examined the barge?' asked Thorndyke.

'Yes. I had a look at it this afternoon. I looked everywhere. The barge is empty. There is nowhere you could hide anything'

'Did you pull the anchor up to look at that?'

'No,' replied Badger. 'I suppose I should have. However, they are pulling it up themselves now.'

We watched through the binoculars. The two passengers were working hard to lift the anchor. When the other two had got the sails ready, they came to help.

'The anchor seems to be very heavy,' said one of the fishermen.

'Yes,' said the other, 'perhaps it is stuck on something under water.'

'Watch the anchor,' said Thorndyke in a low voice.
He kept on looking through his binoculars. 'It is out of
the water — the barge is moving.'

'Where can I get a boat?'

5   As he spoke, we could see the top of the anchor coming
out of the water. Now I could see that there was another
chain fixed to it. Badger had seen it too. In a few
seconds, we could see that there was a box hanging
from the anchor. Badger turned to the two fishermen.
10 'I want a boat. Now. Immediately!' he cried.
The older one of the two looked at him calmly and
replied, 'All right.'
'Where can I get a boat?' Badger asked again. His
face was red with excitement.
15 'Where do you think?' said one of the fishermen. He
was annoyed because Badger was speaking so rudely.
'At a cake shop? Or a garage?'
'Look here,' said Badger, 'I'm a police officer and I
want to go on board that barge. I will pay you well.'
20 'We'll get you on board the barge, if we can catch
it,' replied the fisherman. 'I doubt that we can. It's going
already.' Then he said in a different voice, 'There is
something strange happening on that barge.'
There was. I had been watching it. They got the box
25 on board with some difficulty. Suddenly, a quarrel
began between the two bargemen and their passengers.
Now they were fighting. It was difficult to see exactly
what was happening. The boat was already a long way
down the river. Also, the sail was moving backwards
30 and forwards. In a short while, however, the sails were
filled with wind and a man appeared at the steering
wheel. The barge had a strong wind behind it, and soon
grew small in the distance.

Meanwhile, the fishermen had gone off to find a boat. The inspector stood on the bridge waving his arms and blowing his whistle. Thorndyke continued watching the barge through his binoculars.

I was a little surprised that my friend was not doing anything at all. 'What can we do?' was all he replied. 'Badger will follow the barge. He probably won't catch it. Maybe he can stop them from landing again. He may be able to get some help when he gets out to sea. I think it is all in his hands now.'

Thorndyke said that he would not go with Badger, as it would be an all night trip. 'I must be at work tomorrow morning. Besides, the hunt is not our business. You go if you want to. I can take care of things on my own.'

I decided to go along to see how the matter would end. Thorndyke suggested watching carefully in case the robbers got away. That way, we would at least know where and how they disappeared.

Badger returned with two policemen. They were wearing ordinary clothes. The fishermen had found a boat. When they saw that there were four passengers, they said nothing except to ask if there were any more.

As soon as we sat down, they began rowing, and the village slowly disappeared in the distance. I could still see Thorndyke standing on the bridge watching us.

The barge was already two miles away. It seemed to be going faster than we were, but we could not be sure. The tide was falling, and most of the time we could see only the muddy sides of the river. When we came to a straight part of the river, we could see the sails. Unfortunately, every time we saw them they seemed to be further away.

As the river grew wider, one of the fishermen put up a sail and steered. The other one still kept rowing. We were going a bit faster now, but we still could not catch the other boat.

Finally, one of the fishermen spoke to the Inspector. 'I don't think we can catch her,' he said.

5 'Are you sure?' asked Badger.

'She will go with the tide past the mouth of the river and into the deep water and then she'll be gone.'

'Why can't we do the same?' asked Badger.

'Well, it's like this. They will be able to get there easily
10 enough, but the tide is going to turn very soon. It will have turned before we get to the mouth of the river. Then the sea water will start coming back into the river, and we will have to row against it. They will be gone while we are still trying to get to the open sea. By the
15 time we get out they will be miles away.'

Some very good luck

The fisherman was right. The barge just reached the mouth of the river before the tide turned. Before we got there, however, the water was moving back into the
20 river. Badger cried out in anger. He begged the fishermen to continue. He even promised them all kinds of things. Then he tried to row himself but he did not know anything about it, and fell into the bottom of the boat. Finally, the two fishermen rowed as hard as they
25 could. It seemed to take hours. However, when we finally got past the mouth of the river, the barge could not be seen anywhere.

I felt really sorry for Badger. The mistake he made was a natural one for anyone who was not a sailor. He
30 had been so careful with the other details. His idea of staying in Garbridge was correct. Now it looked as if the thieves and the gold would escape. It was really very bad luck.

'Well,' said the older fisherman, 'they're gone. What do we do now?'

Badger just said that we should go in the direction of London. Maybe we would find some help on the way. Just then we had some very good luck. 5

A small steamboat suddenly came toward us. It was a customs ship. 'Saved!' was all Badger could say.

The two fishermen started rowing again, 10 while Badger shouted like a wild animal. In a few minutes we were beside the steamboat. Badger quickly explained everything, and we were taken on board. The small rowing boat was tied behind, and we went to look for the barge. 15

One of the fishermen described the barge very carefully. He added that her name was the *Bluebell* from Maldon. The name was painted on the side. He also said that the barge was probably close to the north shore.

The officer looked through his binoculars and after a short time he said: 'There's a barge over there. Take
5   a look at it.' He gave the binoculars to the fisherman. After a few moments, this fisherman said that it was probably the one we were looking for. 'It's probably going to Leigh or Southend,' he added. 'Or one of those quiet little bays, to hide the box.'
10   Slowly, the barge came closer. At last we could see the name, *Bluebell*. Badger was happy, and the officer of the boat was smiling.

We catch the criminals

At last we were beside the barge. A sailor threw a rope
15   over to the barge, and two Customs officers, as well as Badger and the two policemen, jumped on board. The two men sailing the barge attempted to fight, but soon they were beaten and taken prisoner. They were then pulled up into the steamboat and guarded. The chief
20   officer, the two fishermen and I then jumped onto the barge and went down into the cabin.

There we saw a curious scene. The captain and his son were tied up. They had a piece of cloth tied over their
25   mouths.

On the table was a small box which looked like the one described on the cargo list. We quickly freed the captain and his son. Two sailors took the box up and carried it to the steamboat.

'Well,' said Badger, drying his face with his handkerchief, 'that ended well enough. I really thought we had lost the men and the gold. What are you going to do? I am going to stay on the boat until we get to the Custom-house in London. If you want to get home sooner, I expect we can let you land at Southend.'

I decided to do this. I went on shore at Southend. There I sent off a telegram from Badger to his office. By then it was quite late in the evening, but I was lucky enough to catch a train to London.

When I arrived at home, Thorndyke was looking through some papers.

'You are back sooner than I expected,' he said. 'How did it go? Did you catch the barge?'

'Yes. We got the men and the gold. But we almost lost both.' Then I told him the rest of the story.

'That steamboat was a bit of good luck. I am glad you caught them. It makes the case so much simpler.'

'It seems to finish the case,' I said. 'We have the stolen gold and the thieves. But Badger did most of the work.'

'Yes, Jervis. I am not jealous. We will go to Police Headquarters in the morning to see if the box is the right one. If it is, the case is finished.'

'It is not really necessary,' I said. 'The marks were all correct. You will see for yourself tomorrow morning. But I suppose you are right to be so careful.'

A big surprise

The next morning, some time after eleven o'clock, we went to Chief Inspector Miller's office at Police

Headquarters. When we came in, Miller looked up. 'I told you Thorndyke would not be satisfied until he had seen everything for himself,' he said to Badger. Badger only smiled at us.

5   'Yes,' said Thorndyke, 'if you don't mind —'

'Not at all. Come along Badger, show him your prize.' We all went into a room, which Miller unlocked. Inside, on a table, was the box. It had not been opened. Thorndyke looked at it closely, and compared the

10   marks on it with his notebook.

'You haven't opened it yet,' said Thorndyke.

'No. You can see that the Customs seals have not been broken,' replied Miller.

'I just thought you might like to know what is inside.'

15   The two officers looked at him. Badger said: 'We know what is inside. It was opened at Customs. There are four gold bars inside.'

'Well,' said Thorndyke, 'as I am working for the Insurance Company, I would like to see what is inside.'

20   Everyone was very surprised. I must admit I did not understand either.

'I have never met such an unbelieving person,' said Miller. 'But if you are not satisfied you may see it.' He looked at Badger. 'Open it and let him see it. I suppose

25   he will want to test the gold afterwards to see how pure it is.'

Miller left and came back in a few minutes with some tools to open the box. This was done very quickly. Inside was some thick cloth which he lifted. We could

30   all see the yellow gold at the top of the box.

'Are you satisfied now? Or do you want to see the other bars underneath?' Miller said to Thorndyke.

Thorndyke pointed to some scales on the table. 'Is that weighing machine a good one?' he asked.

35   'Correct to an ounce,' Miller replied. 'Why?'

Thorndyke did not answer. Instead, he lifted one of the bars out of the box and put it on the machine. Everyone waited.

Lead!

'Twenty-nine pounds and three ounces,' said Thorndyke.

'Well? What about it?' asked Miller.   10

For a moment Thorndyke said nothing. Then he answered in a quiet voice: 'Lead.'

'What!' the two officers cried at the same time and then ran to the scales to take a closer look at the bar of metal. Badger turned and said angrily: 'Nonsense.   15
Look at it. Can't you see it's gold?'

'There is a small amount of gold on the outside,' replied Thorndyke, 'but most of this bar is made of lead.'

'That's impossible. Why do you think it's lead?' asked   20
Miller.

'The volume of this bar is seventy-two cubic inches and it weighs twenty-nine pounds. Physics tells us that it must be a bar of lead. If you don't believe me, it is quite easy to settle the matter. May I cut off a little   25
piece?'

'I suppose so. Yes, all right,' replied Miller.

Thorndyke placed his pocket knife on a corner of the bar. He hit it with a hammer that Miller had brought

in. A little piece fell off. Inside, the colour was grey.
There was no mistake.

'Good Heavens! The thieves have escaped with the
gold after all,' Miller cried. He looked at Thorndyke.
'Unless you know where it is. I expect you do know.'

'I believe I do,' said Thorndyke. 'If you come to the
London Docks with me I think I can hand it over to
you.'

Miller's face grew brighter. Badger's face did not.
'Why didn't you tell us all this before?' he asked. 'You
let me go hunting after that barge, while you knew all
the time the gold was not on it.'

'My dear Badger,' explained Thorndyke. 'Don't you
see that these lead bars were necessary for our case?
They prove that the gold bars were never unloaded.
Therefore they must still be on the ship. This gives us
the right to go on board and take any gold we find in
the ship. If we didn't have these lead bars, we would
not be able to do anything at all.'

'You see, Badger,' said Miller, 'it is no good arguing
with Thorndyke. He can see all around him at once.
Let us go to the docks.'

Just a box of brass bolts

We all left to take the train to the docks. There,
Thorndyke spoke to a Customs officer who hurried
away, and came back with another officer of higher
rank. He said, 'The package you are looking for has
been unloaded. It's in my office. Will you come and
take a look at it?'

In the office, there was a box on a table. This one
was a little larger than the one at Police Headquarters.
There were also some papers.

'I think this is the box,' the officer said. 'But you had better check the cargo list, to see if it agrees. Here it is: "One box containing seventeen and three-quarter dozen brass screws, six inches by three-eighths of an inch. Weight, one hundred and thirteen pounds. Addressed to Jackson and Walker, London". Is that the one?'

'That is the one,' answered Thorndyke.

'Let us open it and look at the brass screws,' said the officer.

The box was quickly opened. Inside was some heavy cloth. The cloth was lifted. Everyone looked. Suddenly Badger's face changed. He looked very disappointed.

'You have missed it this time, Sir,' he said, annoyed. 'This is just a box of brass bolts.'

'Gold bolts,' Thorndyke corrected him. He took one out and gave it to him. 'Did you ever feel a brass bolt this heavy?' he asked.

Badger admitted, 'It certainly is very heavy.' He then handed it to Miller.

'The cargo list says it weighs eight and a half ounces. We will have to check it,' said Thorndyke. He took a small balance from his pocket and weighed it. 'Eight ounces and two-thirds. A brass bolt of the same size would only weigh three ounces and four-fifths. The weight of these bolts comes to one hundred and thirteen pounds. The missing bars weighed one hundred and thirteen pounds and two ounces. It is, therefore, very likely that it is the same gold. They did a very good job of melting them to lose only two ounces. Has the agent of Jackson and Walker come yet?'

'He is waiting outside,' replied the officer with a smile. 'He is getting very impatient. Shall I bring him in?'

The man was brought in. He was small and unhealthy looking. When he saw the open box and all the men in the room, he turned and ran. He ran along the docks as if the devil were chasing him.

How did Thorndyke know?

'Of course, it is all perfectly simple,' I said to Thorndyke when we got home. 'I just don't see how you knew. What made you think the stolen box was a false one?'

'At first,' Thorndyke answered, 'it was only a suspicion. The robbery described by Halethorpe was a very simple job. It was not planned well. When I realized this, I asked myself: what is the right way to steal gold like this?

'The biggest problem is to get the gold away from the scene of the crime. Gold is very heavy. It is, therefore, best to take the gold some time before the crime can be discovered. If you can get someone else to steal a false box, it is even better. By the time the false box is discovered, the real thieves will have had lots of time to get away. And if the false box is not found, the police will never even think of looking in the right direction. The thief who stole the false box of gold will discover the trick when he tries to sell it. But, he cannot complain to the police, as he is a thief himself. That is the correct sort of plan for stealing gold.

'At first there was nothing to suggest that this had happened, but the possibility had to be kept in mind. I knew that we had to make sure the gold bars were still in the box when it left Bellhaven. We had to find someone who actually saw the gold there. That man was Mr Byrne. It was immediately clear to me that the gold bars had already disappeared.

'I calculated the size of the real gold bars. Their volume would be about forty-two cubic inches. Their size should be about seven inches by three by two. The measurements given by Byrne were impossible. The gold bars would have weighed two hundred pounds, instead of one hundred and thirteen. I am surprised Byrne did not notice this. Most Customs officers would have noticed it.'

'Isn't it strange,' I asked, 'that the thieves would take such a chance?'

'I think,' he continued, 'that they did not know what a risk they were taking. Few people realize how strict the Customs are these days.

'It is clear that the bars Byrne examined were not the real ones. The next question was: where were the real ones? That's when I decided to go through the cargo list. I was looking for a parcel that was almost the same weight as the stolen bars. I soon discovered the box of brass screws. Their weight was within two ounces of the gold. Besides, who would send brass bolts from Africa to London?

'This seemed strange. I divided the weight by the number of bolts. Each bolt weighed about half a pound. This meant that they could not be brass, and that they were probably gold.'

'What about the nuts, seeds and the rocks?' I asked.

'I didn't want the man in the shipping agent's office to know what I was doing. It was to deceive him.'

'Then you really had the case solved when we left Bellhaven?'

'In a way, yes. But we still had to find the stolen lead bars. Without them, we could not prove that the bolts
5 were made of the stolen gold. It would be like proving a murder without a body.'

'How do you suppose the robbery was done? How did the thieves get the gold from the ship's strong-room?'

The real thieves

10 'I think it was never there. I suspect the thieves are the ship's first mate, the engineer, and one of the sailors. The mate controls the loading of the cargo. The chief engineer controls the repair shop. He has all the tools necessary for melting the gold. When they heard the
15 gold was coming, they made another box which looked exactly the same, and hid it. As soon as the gold came on board, they exchanged it and took the false one to the strong-room. The real gold was hidden. Later, the engineer would have cut up the gold. He could then
20 melt it and make gold bolts just like he can make brass ones. The mate had lots of time to change the cargo list, and send a bill of lading to a friend in London. This is what I think happened.'

Thorndyke's idea was exactly right. Badger soon
25 caught the agent who had run away. Later, the mate, chief engineer and a sailor on the ship were arrested. When they were tried, they confessed. They described their crime almost exactly as Thorndyke had said it happened.

QUESTIONS AND ACTIVITIES

CHAPTER 1 (A)

Use these words to fill the gaps: **muscle, wrong, suffocate, believe, towards, frightened, stared, covering, hat, breathe, picture, covered, rolled.**

Then I looked again at the (1) _____ of the man with the Spanish (2) _____. There was something (3) _____ with it. Something dark was (4) _____ his face. I (5) _____ onto my back and (6) _____ up. I could not (7) _____ my eyes. Slowly, silently, the top of the bed was coming down (8) _____ me. I was so (9) _____ that I could not move a (10) _____. When it (11) _____ me, I knew that I would not be able to (12) _____. It would (13) _____ me.

CHAPTER 1 (B)

Put the beginnings of these sentences with the right endings.

1 It was too dangerous to escape through the house

2 I ran to a police station and spoke to an officer,

3 Six men got ready, we all went to the house

4 The officers tied up the man who answered the door

5 The 'old soldier' knew about the bed

(a) and when I told him the whole story, he believed me.

(b) and so did the croupier and the woman.

(c) and everyone else in the house was caught too.

(d) so I climbed out of the window.

(e) and an officer knocked on the door.

CHAPTER 2 (A)

Which of these statements about the secret organization are true, and which are false? What is wrong with the false ones?

1 You will know everybody, and they will know you.
2 General meetings are every six months.
3 At the general meetings, everyone wears false beards.
4 Number One knows everything that is happening.
5 There are one hundred members of the organization.
6 All members get an equal share of the money.

CHAPTER 2 (B)

Choose the right words to say what this part of the story is about.

Wimsey asked Number One for a quick (1) **drink/death**. He said he had something to (2) **sell/hide**. He had left a (3) **letter/parcel** with the police which contained the secret (4) **number/word** for the (5) **lock/picture** on his safe. When Number (6) **Fifteen/Sixteen** said that the safe had been (7) **destroyed/searched**, Wimsey (8) **gasped/smiled** and told them about the (9) **outer/inner** room.

CHAPTER 2 (C)

*Who said these words? Choose from: **Inspector Parker, Number One, Number Two, Wimsey (Rogers), Jukes.** You must use some names more than once.*

1 'He must be dead and buried. And I am free!'
2 'We won't quarrel. Will you have a drink with me?'
3 'I will give you some information, but that is all.'
4 'We have a traitor among us. He is here, in this room.'
5 'Quick! I will have it torn out of you — the word!'
6 'He must be saved and only you can do it. Quickly!'
7 'For two years you let us think you were dead.'

CHAPTER 3 (A)

Put these sentences in the right order to say what this part of the story is about. Start with sentence number 1.

1 Sir William opened his parcel and growled angrily.
2 She ate the first one and said the filling was very strong.
3 The doctor saved him, but his wife was already dead.
4 Beresford gave them to his wife just after lunch.
5 A few minutes later, he left to go to a business meeting.
6 Beresford said he had to buy his wife some chocolates.
7 When he arrived at his club, he was almost unconscious.
8 Mason & Sons had sent him a box of new chocolates.
9 Sir William gave his box of chocolates to Beresford.
10 Then Beresford ate one too, and noticed a burning taste.

CHAPTER 3 (B)

Correct the eight errors in these notes from Mrs Verreker's story.

Joan Beresford and I weren't close friends. The worst thing is that she was responsible for her husband's death. If Beresford had won the bet, Sir William would never have eaten the poisoned chocolates. Well, Beresford cheated! She had seen the film before. She went alone, on the first day it came to the theatre. But she did not say so to Sir William.

CHAPTER 4 (A)

*Put these place-names in the right gaps. You will have to use some more than once: **Ancaster, Garbridge, Accra, Bellhaven.***

The gold was put on a ship at (1) _____ and landed safely at the port of (2) _____. Then it was put on the train at (3) _____, and sent to (4) _____, where the factory is. The trains do not go directly from (5) _____ to (6) _____. You have to change trains at (7) _____, a small country station. Here the box was taken out of the train from (8) _____. It had to wait for the train to (9) _____.

CHAPTER 4 (B)

Copy the table and write the answers in the right places. You will see the name of a place in the centre column. Choose from: **water, barge, through, anchor, Badger, chain, banging, heavy, box.**

We watched (1) _____ the binoculars as the men on the (2) _____ worked hard to pull up the (3) _____. It seemed to be very (4) _____. When it came out of the (5) _____, we saw another (6) _____ fixed to it. There was a (7) _____ (8) _____ from it. Excited, (9) _____ asked where he could get a boat.

CHAPTER 4 (C)

Put the words at the end of each sentence in the right order.

1 The barge had a good   [river] [down] [long] [the]
   wind behind it and was   [way].
   soon a

2 When Badger's boat   [be] [could] [barge] [seen]
   reached the sea, the   [not].

3 A Customs ship came   [board] [on] [taken] [were]
   towards them and   [they].

4 When they caught up   [into] [went] [cabin] [down]
   with the barge, Jarvis and [the].
   the others

5 They found a small box   [in] [cargo] [described] [the]
   which looked like the one [list].

CHAPTER 4 (D)

Put the letters of these words in the right order. The first one is 'Headquarters'.

The next morning we went to Police (1) **tHaqueerrads**. We all went into a (2) **moro**, and inside, on a (3) **bleat**, was the box. The (4) **stumsoC slase** had not been broken. He asked to see what was (5) **diseni**. Everyone was very (6) **spurrside**. The box was opened very (7) **klicquy**. Thorndyke (8) **teflid** one of the gold bars out of the box and put it on the (9) **gnewhigi hamicen**. It was (10) **dale**.

GRADE 1

Alice's Adventures in Wonderland
Lewis Carroll

The Call of the Wild and Other Stories
Jack London

Emma
Jane Austen

The Golden Goose and Other Stories
Retold by David Foulds

Jane Eyre
Charlotte Brontë

Just So Stories
Rudyard Kipling

Little Women
Louisa M. Alcott

The Lost Umbrella of Kim Chu
Eleanor Estes

The Secret Garden
Frances Hodgson Burnett

Tales From the Arabian Nights
Edited by David Foulds

Treasure Island
Robert Louis Stevenson

The Wizard of Oz
L. Frank Baum

GRADE 2

The Adventures of Sherlock Holmes
Sir Arthur Conan Doyle

A Christmas Carol
Charles Dickens

The Dagger and Wings and Other Father Brown Stories
G.K. Chesterton

The Flying Heads and Other Strange Stories
Edited by David Foulds

The Golden Touch and Other Stories
Edited by David Foulds

Gulliver's Travels — A Voyage to Lilliput
Jonathan Swift

The Jungle Book
Rudyard Kipling

Life Without Katy and Other Stories
O. Henry

Lord Jim
Joseph Conrad

A Midsummer Night's Dream and Other Stories from Shakespeare's Plays
Edited by David Foulds

Oliver Twist
Charles Dickens

The Mill on the Floss
George Eliot

Nicholas Nickleby
Charles Dickens

The Prince and the Pauper
Mark Twain

The Stone Junk and Other Stories
D.H. Howe

Stories from Greek Tragedies
Retold by Kieran McGovern

Stories from Shakespeare's Comedies
Retold by Katherine Mattock

Tales of King Arthur
Retold by David Foulds

The Talking Tree and Other Stories
David McRobbie

Through the Looking Glass
Lewis Carroll

GRADE 3

The Adventures of Huckleberry Finn
Mark Twain

The Adventures of Tom Sawyer
Mark Twain

Around the World in Eighty Days
Jules Verne

The Canterville Ghost and Other Stories
Oscar Wilde

David Copperfield
Charles Dickens

Fog and Other Stories
Bill Lowe

Further Adventures of Sherlock Holmes
Sir Arthur Conan Doyle

Great Expectations
Charles Dickens

Gulliver's Travels — Further Voyages
Jonathan Swift